Social Studies Comes Alive

For Grades 6–10

Social Studies Comes Alive

Engaging, Effective Strategies for the Social Studies Classroom

R. Casey Davis

Prufrock Press Inc.

Waco, Texas

Acknowledgements

To the Triune God, through whom all things are possible.

To all of my family who believes in me.

To all of the teachers in my life, especially my mom and dad,
Phyllis and Jerry Davis, my mother-in-law, Tawny Lamb, and
sister-in-law, Vanessa Gilbert-Cronen.

To my fellow teachers and all of my students,
thank you for your patience.

To my friends, especially Greg Gallop, BJ Burrow,
Greg Billings, the Brothers Moss, Tim Dayton,
Ronnie Aramas, Clay Thurmond, and everyone
who has accompanied me on this wild ride.

To the staff at Prufrock Press, thank you for taking a chance.

And last, but in no ways least, to Raquel: You are my
soul mate, inspiration, and muse. You look at anything
and tell me I can do it. I love you, eternally.

Library of Congress Cataloging-in-Publication Data

Davis, R. Casey, 1973- author.
 Social studies comes alive : exciting history classroom activities students will love! / By R. Casey Davis.
  p. cm.
 Includes bibliographical references.
 ISBN 978-1-61821-077-7 (pbk.)
 1. Social sciences--Study and teaching (Middle school)--Activity programs. 2. Social sciences--Study and teaching (Secondary)--Activity programs. I. Title.
 H62.5.U5D19 2014
 300.71'273--dc23
          2013046435

Edited by Rachel Taliaferro

Layout and cover design by Raquel Trevino

ISBN-13: 978-1-61821-077-7

Prufrock Press Inc.
P.O. Box 8813
Waco, TX 76714-8813
Phone: (800) 998-2208
Fax: (800) 240-0333
http://www.prufrock.com

Table of Contents

Introduction

This book is intended for preservice and in-service classroom teachers alike. It should not be utilized as "curriculum in a can." In fact, if anyone attempts to do so, the author promises to visit myriad unfortunate circumstances upon those who do (joking).

All of the classroom approaches and activities examined in the chapters came out of my own desperation and boredom, and they are activities that I shared with my students over the years as a middle school social studies teacher. Granted, there is a certain level of foundational knowledge and skill set that the students must master. However, even I went through high school and into college thinking that all there was to social studies, especially history, was memorizing dates and coloring maps. It wasn't until I mustered out of the Army and returned to school that I learned there was so much more to learning and teaching this wonderful field, thanks to Dr. Paul Travis at Texas Woman's University in Denton, TX. He was more than a professor and a degree advisor to me. He was my mentor and a sage who taught me the possibilities of the classroom.

The primary goals of these activities and approaches are to generate an authentic interest in social studies among students. Many times when students matriculate to middle school grades, their interest in social studies dwindles or completely disappears. When I informally surveyed my own students as to why this occurred, the majority responded that they were bored with the class because of the way it was taught. It was no longer interesting. The majority of the students saw social studies as "just a bunch of dead people." Students had a difficult time relating to the material, let alone seeing that they were contributing to the continuing narrative of history.

With the cognitive and developmental levels of students in these grades, it is not surprising that these reactions to and challenges in teaching social studies arise. Added to this is the difficulty brought about by the instantaneous nature of today's technology-based culture. These approaches and activities can help to redirect the waning attention span and interest of the students, and even begin to develop student-directed learning within the social studies classroom.

Although each chapter has a specific section for suggested student products, each chapter also comes with a handout that lists product options for the students to choose from that I've used in my own classrooms. This should provide plenty of choices for teachers, especially if they are catering to a differentiated classroom. The classroom activities and student products included in the individual chapters are meant to engage and excite the students in the classroom. The examples included in the chapters and handouts are just that, examples. They can be implemented, but are meant to give teachers an idea of how to effectively utilize the approach, activities, and products. Feel free to adapt them according to your own resources and classroom needs. These approaches and activities only have two limits on them. They are the time limits enforced by the campus or district's scope and sequence and the teacher's imagination and ingenuity. Otherwise, the sky's the limit.

At the end of each chapter is an annotated bibliography that lists suggested books and websites for use in the classroom or to recommend to students for further study. In the appendix at the end of the book (p. 121) is a general scoring rubric—along with explanations and definitions of the scoring criteria and the terms used in the rubric—that can be adapted to assess the student products suggested in each chapter. I have used the instructional approaches, classroom activities, student products, and the assessment rubric in my classroom in the years that I have taught social studies as well as English/language arts and science. I have been able to adapt them easily to fit the content matter and grade levels. My sincere hope is that they will serve you and your students as well as they have mine.

Chapter 1

Folklore in the Classroom

Introduction

We all love stories. Stories are both magical and memorable. They can simultaneously make time stop and fast-forward. In our era of instant information and gratification, the dwindling art of storytelling is rapidly becoming extinct. This is a sad fact especially in the classroom. From the beginning of time, humans have taught using stories as the vehicles for communicating knowledge and wisdom passed down through the ages. This diminished with the advent of writing, the printing press, broadcast communications, and now digital information. However, this particular instructional approach helps to revive folklore and folk wisdom.

Folklore defines a place and culture as much as any other artifact. Although locating the distinctive marks of each generation may be somewhat more difficult than with a physical artifact, it is not completely impossible. Locating the unique geographic impressions and nuances of folklore's origin and travels can be ascertained through careful study. One of the main attractions of this particular instructional approach and its subsequent activity is the connections students can make with their community through the product options.

First, we need to arrive at a working definition as to what folklore is. For the purposes of this instructional approach, folklore can be understood as the collected wisdom and knowledge of a particular culture and/or society unique to a particular historical era located in a particular geographic region or location. Although there will be evidence of cultural sharing and diffusion of certain folklore, we will concentrate on individual people, places, and times before making connections with others.

There are two legitimate academic disciplines from which social studies teachers can draw both inspiration and direction when preparing and implementing this approach: cultural anthropology and comparative literature. These two disciplines have seen healthy growth in the past few decades, and practitioners are utilizing new approaches, techniques, and methodologies for analyzing and critiquing their studies. Perusing some of the latest studies and articles dedicated to these fields may be of great help to the teacher.

Folklore in the Classroom

Before launching into the activity itself, let's look at an example of folklore and how it might be applied to a secondary social studies classroom. One of the more widely recognized pieces of world literature is *The Epic of Gilgamesh*. The majority of students and teachers have at least heard of this legend in name, even if they are not familiar with the story. There are numerous translations and retellings of this ageless classic. A brief Internet search will assist the teacher in locating not only a suitable version of the story, but also a downloadable one as well to save money. One of the better URLs to find a copy of this is http://www.gutenberg.org/ebooks/11000. This is a digital copy of the text found at Project Gutenberg. Utilizing this particular copy removes any of the copyright issues that classroom teachers may encounter. Also, having access to a digital copy allow the teachers to print off copies, print off only the portions they wish to use, post the link on their websites, and even encourage digital reading.

It is highly recommended that the classroom teacher commit to a close reading of this tale before guiding the students through the activity. Teachers should read the story once to ascertain a feel for the geography of the story, and a second time to immerse themselves in the details and nuances of the ancient epic from the Middle East. Doing this will help alleviate quite a bit of frustration later when the teacher holds class discussions and presents the students with their assignments.

The Internet is home to a plethora of essays and study guides posted by professors and scholars of classical and world literature to aid the social studies teacher implementing this activity. I also suggest inviting the assistance of a colleague from the English/language arts department. Not only is this a great means of collaboration, but it also is a strong way of building a team within the campus.

Once the classroom teacher is comfortable enough, or it is time to have the students begin their immersion in the piece of folklore, the first step needs to be an exploration of the geographic region or place where the folklore originated. This is important, as it is very rare that a story's physical location does not leave its own indelible stamp upon the folklore. From Native American to Norse, the

> ➤ 3–5 days: Build foundational knowledge of the geographic region to include historic and cultural background.
>
> ➤ 5–10 days: Read *The Epic of Gilgamesh*. (This can be easily shortened by assigning reading outside of class.)
>
> ➤ 2–3 days: Students create their projects.
>
> ➤ 1–2 days: Student present their products.
>
> **FIGURE 1.1.** Suggested timeline.

folklore from aboriginal cultures is shaped by the location where the cultures created it. It shows the intimate relationship that people had and have with the environment they live in.

Classroom Activity

Utilizing *The Epic of Gilgamesh* in the social studies classroom seems like a readymade relationship. It is a wonderful instrument for classroom use because it is fairly easy for students to interpret and can be made as complex as the teacher wishes. From these vantage points, *The Epic of Gilgamesh* can be considered something of an exemplar of folklore. Studying this aspect of culture is usually reserved for university-level classes, but in this case can be easily and effectively adapted for middle school students.

After a quick review or study of the history and geography of the region, the teacher can guide the students through a reading of the piece. A suggested timeline can be found in Figure 1.1.

One of the more powerful instructional tools teachers can employ is that of asking guiding questions (see Figure 1.2 for samples). The teacher should assign no more than three questions per reading portion to help guide the students through the passages. Although these are not meant to necessarily directly influence the students' understanding or point of view, they are meant to assist the students in gaining a deeper and richer understanding of the text.

Most social studies teachers will not have the luxury of being able to guide the students through multiple close readings. As such, the teacher will need to guide the students through a multilayered reading. Again, our colleagues in the English/language arts departments are a boon in helping students achieve this particular form of reading awareness. Given the length of the reading, it may actually be advisable for the teacher to initially incorporate excerpts rather than trying to tackle the entire piece, depending on how much class time the teacher has.

> ➤ "Where do you see the influences of geography in this section?"
>
> ➤ "How is this story unique to the region?"
>
> ➤ "Why does this story need to take place here and now?"
>
> ➤ "Could it be placed somewhere else and at another time?"
> _____
> **FIGURE 1.2**. Sample guiding questions.

These guiding questions and the ensuing whole-class discussion lead to more individual reading and group discussions. This second phase of the reading and analysis should be given approximately the same amount of time as the prior portion. As the students show advancing mastery, they need to be guided from collaborative groups to individual reading and analysis before moving to the end product.

Products

The final product is one that challenges the students to produce and perform as closely to the professional level as possible. This addresses the majority of the state and national standards, as well as the college readiness standards in place. This particular instructional approach offers the students two options for the final product, as will the majority of the instructional approaches in this text. This is done to allow the students to explore their strengths and challenge them to examine new areas where they may not have ventured to before.

The first option is the more traditional and familiar product for most students: creating and composing an extended essay or research paper. The student who selects this option is either assigned a topic or selects one. It is recommended that the teacher develop topics that are tied with the region, era, or cultures being studied, or tied in with the local community if possible. This is a powerful way for cultivating stronger ties with the surrounding community and developing resources outside of the campus.

In the paper, the students need to answer the fundamental questions posed when the initial reading was done earlier with *The Epic of Gilgamesh*. However, further research must also be conducted to see what past academics have discovered through their own research and analysis. The goals of this option are to have students generate new analyses, as well as sharpen their research and writing skills. Although the traditional product is very much a viable option, it is recommended that the classroom teacher try to get the students not to rely on it too much.

The second option is more creative: The students will generate their own unique and original piece of folklore. This piece of folklore will originate from the geographic region, historical era, and specific culture or society assigned by the classroom teacher. Otherwise, the students may also select to have the piece of folklore represent the local community. This piece of folklore can be presented in a variety of media. The students, after presenting the piece of folklore, must decode and deconstruct it to show its ties to the region, people, and era for the class. This is their analysis.

There are also other products that are available to students as well. For this particular classroom activity and approach, student products are not limited to the two options listed in the previous paragraphs. Handout 1.1 lists several other options for products, including creating an original piece of folklore from an invented or imagined civilization. In fact, the products are truly only limited by the imagination and ingenuity of the students and the teacher involved. The two options are merely starting points for the students and teachers to begin exploring and discussing what they believe would be an appropriate and fitting product for the literature piece and student population.

Assessment

Regarding assessing the students' products, it is highly recommended that the classroom teacher implement and utilize rubrics. Rubrics are an effective means of removing many judgment errors in portions of subjective grading. A general rubric that may be adapted to fit each chapter's products can be found in the appendix of this book (p. 121). Definitions and explanations for each of the criteria in the general rubric are also provided. The rubric should be shared with the students as soon as the project is assigned to them. The rubric and project should be explained with the whole class in order to alleviate as many misunderstandings and misinterpretations as possible.

Handout 1.1
Folklore in the Classroom

Select a piece of folklore from a particular region/era/culture and analyze it using the following two-step process:

Step 1

Examine the piece of folklore and see if you can fully answer the following questions:

- ❖ What does this piece tell you about the people who created it?
- ❖ What does it tell you about the time in which it was created?
- ❖ What does it tell you about the place where it was created?
- ❖ How does it serve as an example to explain this particular culture/society in this time and place?

Step 2

Using the answers and understanding from Step 1, select one of the three options to complete the analysis of the folklore:

Option 1: Recreate the piece of folklore in modern times in order to reflect the time, place, and culture in which you live.

Option 2: Create an original piece of folklore from the same time, place, and culture that the original piece originated from.

Option 3: Create an original piece of folklore from a completely new and unique civilization that you have created.

Option 4: Write an extended research paper or essay that focuses on a specific civilization's folklore.

Format(s):

When completing Step 2 of the analysis, you are only limited by your imagination in completing the piece. Some more popular formats include graphic novels, comic strips, videos, dramatic monologues, as well as others . . . ***Go forth and create!***

Annotated Bibliography

Dobie, J. F. (1985). *Apache gold & Yaqui silver*. Austin: University of Texas Press. (Work originally published in 1939)

Abstract: In this text, Dobie explores the many legends, rumors, and stories surrounding the gold and silver that came out of the southwestern United States and northern Mexico.

Dobie, J. F. (1978). *Coronado's children: Tales of lost mines and buried treasures of the Southwest*. Austin: University of Texas Press. (Work originally published in 1930)

Abstract: Dobie collects the oral histories, traditions, and folklore from the region comprised of the American Southwest and northern Mexico. This region was widely explored by the Spanish conquistador Francisco Vásquez de Coronado, whose legacy continues today.

Dobie, J. F. (1980). *The longhorns*. Austin: University of Texas Press. (Work originally published in 1941)

Abstract: The book collects the native wisdom and folklore from the American Southwest including collected oral histories from cowboys, ranchers, vaqueros, desperados, Native Americans, and lawmen.

Chapter 2

Geographic Memoirs

Introduction

Most of us are familiar with the term *geography*. We all had to take the class in school. Most of us have either read or seen a memoir. Yet, putting together geography and memoirs is an effective means of teaching students from various and diverse populations to understand two of the most difficult of the five themes of geography: human-environment interaction and place (see Figure 2.1 for a breakdown of the five themes).

Although human-environment interaction and place may seem like simple themes at first glance, they are actually quite difficult to teach to students, even at the secondary level. What is even more difficult to achieve is an effective means of teaching in a cross-curricular or interdisciplinary manner in the social studies classroom. Utilizing geographic memoirs incorporates knowledge and skills from the content areas of science and English/language arts into the social studies classroom.

Before the implementation is completely examined, a better understanding of exactly what a geographic memoir is needs to be established. At the end of this chapter is an annotated bibliography with some suggested texts. For this particular chapter, one of the suggested texts is John Graves' *Goodbye to a River.* This seemingly forgotten contemporary classic of Texana chronicles Graves's trip down a large portion of the Brazos River in late 1960 prior to the construction of the Possum Kingdom Dam. Along the way, Graves intermingles memories, science, folklore, and history with his travelogue.

Five Themes of Geography

➢ Place
   o This theme describes an area using the human inhabitants and physical characteristics.

➢ Location
   o This theme describes where something can be found. There are two different types of location. These are:
   • *relative location*, which describes where a place is in relation to other places and landmarks, and
   • *exact location*, which describes where a place is using descriptors such as latitude and longitude.

➢ Region
   o This theme divides the world into more manageable pieces for study. The theme of region is divided into three different types. These are:
   • *formal regions*, which are described by officially recognized boundaries,
   • *functional regions*, which are described by the connections humans have with it, and
   • *vernacular regions*, which are commonly understood regions such as "New England" and "Latin America."

➢ Human-Environment Interaction
   o This theme is one students find easiest to learn and teachers to explain in the classroom. This theme is focuses on how humans interact with their physical surroundings and how both are changed through these interactions.

➢ Movement
   o This theme looks at the different types of movement such as migration, immigration, and emigration. It also focuses on how people, ideas, and practices move from one place to another.

FIGURE 2.1. Five themes of geography.

This piece of writing, which was originally intended to be a piece of long-form journalism for *Sports Illustrated*, exemplifies what a geographic memoir is supposed to be. Luckily for us, the magazine rejected the piece due to its lack of sporting content, but a book publisher jumped on it instead. Graves utilizes his accumulated wisdom from years of schooling and those passed down to him from his family and friends to enlighten those willing to listen to his words and the spaces between them. The book can be understood as an accumulation of knowledge and wisdom from centuries of lifetimes handed down to the reader.

The following is an example of how Graves expertly weaves the disciplines of the humanities and the sciences. Utilized within an engaging lesson, this text is a veritable gold mine.

> In the yard around his baroque Victorian house he has shrubs transplanted from the Hermitage, and a pecan grown from a nut picked up at Governor Hogg's grave, and roses from cuttings at the site of the cabin his grandfather built east of the town in the 1850's. Not many people like him will still be among us in the next few years. In this country they are mostly of the South and New England, retrospective cultures, and the time has lurched upon the horizon, as it must inevitably for the retrospective cultures, when South and New England will not exist. (p. 57)

Although this does give a glimpse of what constitutes a geographic memoir, it does not necessarily define one. A geographic memoir is a work of literature. This includes prose, poetry, drama, even music. These works of nonfiction establish the location, region, or the place at the central role as the main characters in these literary works. They fit into the newer genre that bears the name of "creative nonfiction" or "literary nonfiction." Utilizing these works in the social studies classroom is not only a way of differentiating for students, but a healthy means of helping our colleagues in the English/language arts department, as many of the state and national standards now specifically list this genre.

Graves uses his ambling journey down the Brazos to literally say his goodbyes to the river that he has known for most of his life. Having spent all of his childhood and decades of his adulthood either alongside or on the river itself, he realizes it will be indelibly changed once the dam is constructed. Although this may seem like an inconsequential event in today's world, it is actually quite the game changer. We now know from modern science that shifting the flow of a river changes both the riverine and the surrounding ecosystems. The far-reaching effects of these changes are just now beginning to be understood. However, Graves understood the emotional and personal repercussions of building the dam and irreversibly changing the river.

> Before leaving, I paddled over up Ioni to the crossing where Jesse Veale died. It is still there, though dozed out for present ranch use; I looked for the old double elm's stump, not remembering whether I'd actually seen it when young or only had seen a photograph, but however that may have been, it was no longer there. Mesquites stand thick on the flat above the crossing now, though probably in the old days they didn't; like cedar, they move onto overused land. Except for a few birds, it was a silent place. (p. 89)

Geographic Memoirs in the Classroom

In a geographic memoir, if it is written well, the voice of the author should easily merge with the voice of the land or place that he or she is writing about. The personality of that place should come through. For more on this particular approach, see the chapter on looking at architecture throughout history.

When the author of a geographic memoir effectively lends his or her voice to a particular region or place, then the land and its flora and fauna can speak, sharing their accumulated experience and wisdom. The human element is never removed from the text. What occurs is a blurring between humans and nature. Through the author's words, the place evokes its own distinctive personality, leaving an indelible impression on the reader. As such, the reader is left with a deeper and more complex understanding of the themes of human-environment interaction and place within the context of geography.

It is highly recommended that the social studies teacher read a geographic memoir at least once before attempting to implement this instructional approach. The campus librarian is an invaluable resource in locating an effective title to use. Once a title has been located and selected, it is time to read and reread. As discussed in the first chapter, the classroom teacher should read the selected text at least twice. The first read should be done for exploration and hopefully enjoyment. The second reading should be done with teaching in mind. This means that the teacher needs to read with the eye of a writer, a critic, and an instructor.

Classroom Activity

Looking at the scope and sequence, as well as his or her pacing guide, the classroom teacher should make the decision before assigning the text as to whether the entire text will be read or taught in excerpts according to his or her own time limitations.

Once the students have the material in front of them, the teacher should ease them into a tiered approach to social studies. The teacher can utilize guiding questions such as:

❖ "Where are the connections between the author/narrator and the place?"
❖ "How does the author/narrator evoke a sense of place through his or her writing?"
❖ "What does the author/narrator do to place the reader into the story with him or her?"

The students will then read over the selected text. Whether they do this individually, in groups, or as a whole group is entirely up to the teacher's discretion and resources.

Student Products

After the students have completed their reading of the piece, then it is time to have them generate original, professional-level products to communicate their mastery of the knowledge and skills. As with the previous chapter in this book, this particular classroom instructional approach offers two options to the students. The first is the more traditional and familiar of the two. Although it is acceptable for the students to select this option, it is advisable for the classroom teacher to encourage and guide the students to not rely upon it too readily.

The first option is the extended essay or research paper. In this option, the students will analyze and deconstruct the geographic memoir that has either been assigned to them by the teacher or one that they have chosen from an approved list compiled by the teacher. The title being analyzed is tied to the geographic region, historical era, or particular culture or society being studied at the time according to the assigned curricular framework of the school district. The primary focus of the students' essays or research papers is to show the human-environment interaction and sense of place as related in the geographic memoir. In order to do this successfully, the students will need to explore not only the assigned or selected piece of literature, but also research other pieces written about the location and region. Reading additional pieces written by the same author, if they are available, will also be of use.

The second option is somewhat more nontraditional and creative in nature. The students create an original piece of geographic memoir based on their own experiences in and around the school. This piece will help the students develop a more reflective and personal writing style. Not only will it challenge the students to think more about their school and physical campus in a practical and physical manner, but also in a figurative and geographical manner. Many students have been at their particular school campus for more than a year. As such, they have attached unique and personal memories to physical aspects of the buildings that comprise the campus.

Making the connection between the physical and personal is a means of making the connections between the concrete and the abstract. Guiding students in this type of learning is visceral and vital. Although this can be difficult for many, the outcome will be positive for the majority. The classroom teacher must proceed with caution and patience when implementing this particular instructional approach and activity.

Once the students have generated their original geographic memoir, it is time for them to present their pieces. It is recommended that this take the shape of a book presentation that professional authors do with the release of a new title. The students should have the chance to read a portion of their work, discuss the writing of it, and field questions. All of this is, of course, under the guidance of classroom teacher. These presentations can be done in a traditional manner or using technology and a variety of media. Handout 2.1 offers a variety of format suggestions, including comic strips and dramatic monologues.

Another option that is available with technology is to have students generate a geographic memoir through social media. Although this will take some prior set-up and clearance regarding security and student protection, most campuses and districts already have numerous safeguards and security restrictions in place for student electronic safety. These geographic memoirs can take the form of a blog, a website, or even Twitter feeds over the course of the unit, grading period, or even the semester. All of this is dependent upon the comfort level of the classroom teacher and the ability of the students.

Even if the teacher is not necessarily completely comfortable with the utilization of technology, teaming up with the campus technologist and/or computer teacher is an instrumental means of generating an interdisciplinary approach to this particular activity. Perhaps the greatest benefit of doing this is that it will capitalize on the students' familiarity with technology, but will also challenge the students to work and generate a product that parallels what they will experience in the professional work environment.

Assessment

When assessing these presentations and products, it is highly recommended that the classroom teacher utilize a rubric to measure student achievement. Feel free to adapt the general rubric provided in the appendix at the end of the book. The rubric should be given to the students when the assignment is given and discussed alongside it.

Handout 2.1
Geographic Memoirs

Select a geographic memoir from a particular region/era/culture and analyze it using the following two-step process:

Step 1

Examine the geographic memoir and see if you can fully answer the following questions:

- ❖ What does this piece tells you about the author's interaction with his or her surroundings?
- ❖ What does it tell you about the time in which it was created?
- ❖ What does it tell you about the particular place?
- ❖ How does it serve as an example of a deep map?

Step 2

Using the answers and understanding from Step 1, select one of the three options to complete the analysis of the geographic memoir:

Option 1: Recreate the geographic memoir in modern times in order to reflect the time, place, and culture in which you live.

Option 2: Create an original geographic memoir from the same time, place, and culture that the original piece originated from.

Option 3: Create an original geographic memoir from a completely new and unique perspective/point of view.

Option 4: Write an extended research paper or essay that analyzes and deconstructs a chosen or assigned geographic memoir.

Format(s)

When completing Step 2 of the analysis, you are only limited by your imagination in completing the piece. Some more popular formats include graphic novels, comic strips, videos, dramatic monologues, as well as others...*Go forth and create!*

Annotated Bibliography

Abbey, E. (1985). *Desert solitaire: A season in the wilderness*. New York, NY: Ballantine. (Work originally published in 1968)

Abstract: From the writer credited with creating the term "eco-terrorism" comes a resonating book born from his time working in Moab, UT. More than anything, Abbey excels at examining human-environment interaction especially at the singular level. In this particular work, the setting is the main character.

Bedichek, R. (1975). *Adventures with a Texas naturalist*. Austin: University of Texas Press. (Work originally published in 1947)

Abstract: This is a rare gem of a book. It is a literate and highly readable text that combines science, natural history, folklore, as well as plentiful references to classical literature. Yet, Bedicheck grounds all of his writing solidly to his native state.

Graves, J. (2002). *Goodbye to a river*. New York, NY: Vintage. (Work originally published in 1960)

Abstract: In this unique book, Graves records his 1960 trip down the Brazos River before the Possum Kingdom Dam is constructed. This text meanders through history, geography, sports, and personal memory as Graves canoes down the Brazos.

Chapter 3

Graphic Storytelling

Introduction

Comic books, comic strips, graphic novels, and manga are everywhere today. Whether in print, animated, or digital formats, there is no denying the infusion of this storytelling format in today's culture. As pervasive and popular as it is, the power that it holds over adolescents and adults alike is mesmerizing. Instead of fighting this continuing trend and tradition of adolescence, many schools have come to embrace and utilize it to enhance classroom instruction.

Although the majority of the instructional activities in this text have solely focused on social studies, this particular activity expands to incorporate numerous disciplines. In fact, this particular instructional approach and activity is perhaps more product-oriented than any of the others examined in this book. Of course, there is the requisite amount of research and some writing involved in this unit. The majority of the work done by the students will be focused on reading and producing their own comic books in class.

Before delving into the actual creation and construction of the comic books, a little background on the medium is called for. Comic books are not a new art form within the scope of human history. Certain links can be made between these often-dismissed publications and with what archaeologists have discovered in the tombs of ancient Egypt and even on the cave walls of Lascaux, France. Humans have been communicating graphically for millennia. It is not too far of a leap to make from graphic to linguistic communication. This connection is one still being researched by anthropologists, linguists, as well as neurologists and geneticists, among other scientists.

Graphic Storytelling in the Classroom

Utilizing comic books, comic strips, manga, and graphic novels in the classroom cannot be done in a haphazard manner. The first means of effectively addressing this implementation for any classroom teacher can be somewhat time consuming but are vitally necessary in order for the teacher to successfully guide the students. Currently, these fields are awash in titles to choose from. The trick is finding one that speaks to the students as well as passes the scrutiny of local school administrators. Luckily, there are some that have been recognized by leading literature organizations—*Maus* by Art Spiegelman, for example.

Establishing a time for teaching and reading these works will differ from class to class, as well as title to title. Utilizing Spielgeman's *Maus* as an example, a sample timeline for implementing this instructional approach is fairly simple and is illustrated in Figure 3.1 on the next page. It could be accomplished in approximately 4 weeks.

The initial step is taking the time to read graphic novels. Just as with any content area, the teacher needs to be very familiar with the instructional tools, information, and the skills they expect to use and the students to pick up through the class. In order for the students to achieve this, the classroom teacher needs to read comic books, comic strips, manga, and graphic novels. The greater the diversity of titles and subject matter, the better prepared the classroom teacher will be to assist the students creating their own graphic narratives in the social studies classroom.

While reading the graphic narratives, the teacher should pay attention to many aspects of this particular medium. As we read these pieces, we need to read them with two different sets of eyes. We must read them with the eyes of everyday devotees and the eyes of a creator, someone who writes and draws graphic narratives everyday. This second way of reading these graphic narratives is more challenging and will take more time to develop, but is well worth the time and effort in order to implement this instructional activity and the eventual student product.

While reading graphic narratives, the teacher should study how the writer and artist convey the story through the combination of verbal and visual storytelling. How do color and the arrangement of the panels help the flow of the narrative? Look at how literally the point of view and perspective of each and every panel on the page adds to the overall story.

Figure 3.2 is a working checklist of what the classroom teacher needs to look for in reviewing graphic novels for use with students.

Once the classroom teacher has broken down the graphic narrative into these separate parts, then it is time to take a step back and look at the entire

Week 1: Introduce the topic. Guide the students in exploring the focus of the graphic novel. In this case, the classroom teacher would introduce and lead an exploration on topics such as genocide and the Holocaust. These explorations go as deep as the students are ready for.

Week 2: This would be the first actual week of reading the text. As with any other classroom reading assignment, the text can be assigned for both in-class as well as out-of-class reading. The most important aspect of this reading is getting students to interact with and relate to the text.

Week 3: This week is a continuation of assigned reading. One of the more effective tools to guiding students in making connections with the text is using a reader response journal. This is basically having students reflect on what they have read. Guided questions assist students in thinking and reflecting on the assigned reading.

Week 4: This portion of time would be used to wrap up any unfinished reading as well as for working on the project.

FIGURE 3.1. Sample timeline.

❏ **Support of established learning standards:** The teacher must ensure that everything brought into the classroom supports the standards and the test(s) as strongly as possible.

❏ **Suitability for students:** The teacher must ensure that the selection is as appropriate as possible for the cognitive levels of the students while challenging them at the same time. The piece must also meet the appropriate expectations of what students need to read.

❏ **Balance of education and entertainment:** Any graphic novel utilized in the classroom must strike as close to an optimal balance between entertainment and educational information.

❏ **Interdisciplinary inclinations:** A graphic novel used in the classroom should ideally address two or more content areas for more in-depth and complex engagement.

❏ **Differentiation:** The graphic novel should lend itself to being used across a great population of students with different ability levels.

FIGURE 3.2. Graphic novel checklist.

piece as whole. Examine the graphic narrative as a single piece and see how the storytelling was achieved. In this portion, the teacher takes on the role of not only a writer and artist of graphic narratives, but also a critic. Once the classroom teacher feels confident in reading graphic narratives in this manner, it is time to proceed to instructing the students and implementing this particular instructional activity.

Classroom Activity

When introducing this activity and approach to the students, the teacher will want to follow the same process he or she did in familiarizing him or herself with graphic narratives. According to however much time is allotted the particular unit of study, the teacher can appropriate enough class time for students to become familiar with comic books, comic strips, graphic novels, and manga in order to be ready to dive into a more critical level of reading these pieces.

At this second level, the classroom teacher needs to guide the students into thinking critically and creatively at the same time. Having gone through a similar experience will help the classroom teacher effectively guide the students through this phase of the instructional activity. While the students are reading these pieces critically, they should also have already been assigned or have selected the topic that they will be generating their own graphic narrative on. This topic will ideally come from the historical era or geographic region being studied, but Figure 3.3 offers some sample topics. This way the students can consider how they would want their own pieces to be constructed as they read.

Student Products

This leads us to the actual product. The students will be creating their own graphic story. The script that they will create will come from a primary source, such as a letter, journal entry, or even a well-known public document that is relevant to their topic. As such, the students will not necessarily have the pressure of creating a historically accurate story from scratch. What the students will be responsible for is arranging the primary source in a script and laying it out before generating an original graphic narrative. Handout 3.1 offers some guiding questions and format suggestions.

Students will need to consider, under the guidance of the classroom teacher, the number of panels per page, the number of pages, and other facets of graphic narratives that add up to major components in the end. Figure 3.4 is an example of what blank cells typically look like, although students can adapt the sizing and shape of the cells according to how they want to tell their story. Figure 3.5 provides a sample script with illustration directions This will help both the

- ➢ The Crusades
- ➢ Building the Roman Empire
- ➢ China Explores the World
- ➢ The Space Race
- ➢ Cortés Comes to America
- ➢ Squanto and the Pilgrims
- ➢ Newton's New Idea

FIGURE 3.3. Sample topics.

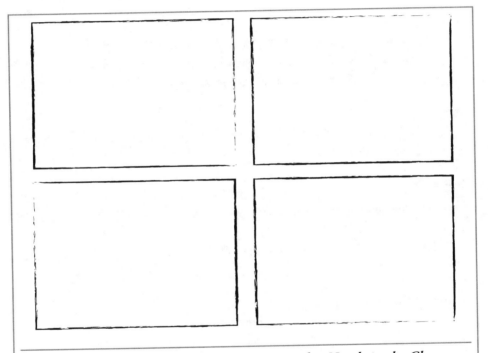

FIGURE 3.4. Blank cells. From *Teaching Graphic Novels in the Classroom: Building Literacy and Comprehension* (p. 143), by R. Novak, Waco, TX: Prufrock Press. Copyright 2014 by Prufrock Press. Reprinted with permisson.

classroom teacher and the students have an idea of what the script should look like when they are creating their own graphic narratives from primary source documents.

At the end of the unit, the students should turn in the script, with corrections and rewrites, along with the completed graphic narrative. This script serves as a guide and framework allowing the students and teachers to see the process

Sample Script

Panel 1

A large group of birds (you decide the number) are taking flight

Narrator:

Being able to fly like a bird is a dream of many

Panel 2:

A young boy (modeled however you want) stands with his hands on his hips in his best Superman pose. He is wearing pajamas with a blanket tied around his neck, like a cape.

Narrator:

As children, we all dreamed of it.

Panel 3:

A frog sits on the ground stairing up at birds taking flight. He looks sad

Narrator:

But humans are not the only ones who have this dream

Panel 4:

The frog daydreams of being able to fly. His thought balloon has an image of him taking flight with birds wings sprouting from his back

Panel 5:

The frog now looks happy

frog:

I'm gonna fly like the birds!

Panel 6:

A group of birds are standing nearby and overhear him.

Bird 1:

You're a frog, stupid! frogs can't fly!

Other birds:

Hahahaha!

Panel 7:

The frog again looks sad

frog (sadly):

I'll prove them wrong

FIGURE 3.5. Sample Script. From *Teaching Graphic Novels in the Classroom: Building Literacy and Comprehension* (p. 143), by R. Novak, Waco, TX: Prufrock Press. Copyright 2014 by Prufrock Press. Reprinted with permisson.

used to arrive at the finished piece. The second portion will be the final, illustrated graphic narrative.

Assessment

It is highly recommended that the classroom teacher utilize a rubric when assessing the students' products to measure achievement. Rubrics need to be shared with the students when the project is originally assigned in order to alleviate as many misunderstandings as possible at the beginning. Because the product in this chapter requires significant artwork, strive to be as objective as possible in assessing the students' work—try to focus on creativity over technical quality.

Handout 3.1
Graphic Storytelling

Select a comic book, graphic novel, manga, or comic strip and analyze it using the following two-step process:

Step 1

Examine the piece and see if you can fully answer the following questions:
* ❖ What does this piece tell you about the people who created it?
* ❖ What does it tell you about the time in which it was created?
* ❖ What does it tell you about the place where it was created?
* ❖ How does it serve as an example to explain this particular culture/society in this time and place?

Step 2

Using the answers and understanding from Step 1, select one of the three options to complete the analysis of the graphic storytelling:

Option 1: Recreate the piece in your context.
Option 2: Create an original piece from the same time, place, and culture that the original piece originated from.
Option 3: Create an original piece from a completely new and unique civilization that you have created.

Format(s)

When completing Step 2 of the analysis, formats include graphic novels, comic strips, manga, illustrated dramatic monologues, as well as others . . . ***Go forth and create!***

Annotated Bibliography

Neufeld, J. (2010). *A.D.: New Orleans after the deluge*. New York, NY: Pantheon.

Abstract: Josh Neufeld's graphic novel follows with tender honesty the lives of a handful of Hurricane Katrina survivors years after the storm. Based on interviews and supported by realistic artwork, this work will not stop short of stunning the students.

Novak, R. (2014). *Teaching graphic novels in the classroom: Building literacy and comprehension*. Waco, TX: Prufrock Press.

Abstract: Author Ryan Novak describes in his book different methods teachers may use to begin teaching graphic literature in the classroom. The last chapter is the culminating project for the book and should be particularly useful here—it guides students creating their own graphic novel through the writing and artistic processes.

Santiago, W. (2011). *21: The story of Roberto Clemente*. New York, NY: Fantagraphics.

Abstract: This amazing piece of graphic storytelling by Wilfred Santiago about Puerto Rican baseball player Roberto Clemente will appeal to a wide variety of students. The story and artwork are an immediate appeal, given the centrality of sports to the narrative.

Sax, A. (2013). *The war within these walls*. Grand Rapids, MI: Eerdmans.

Abstract: Narrated by teenage Misha, this graphic novel by Aline Sax blends art and history to tell the story of Misha's struggle in Nazi-occupied Poland.

Spiegelman, A. (1996). *Maus: A survivor's tale*. New York, NY: Pantheon.

Abstract: This Pulitzer Prize-winning graphic novel by Art Spiegelman tells the story of Vladek Spiegelman, a Jewish survivor of the Holocaust, and his son, a cartoonist struggling to make an effort to connect with his father. The iconic artwork and poignancy of the story can be put to excellent use in the social studies or history classroom.

Sturm, J. (2007). *Satchel Paige: Striking out Jim Crow*. New York, NY: Hyperion.

Abstract: James Sturm's graphic novel is a powerful text to have as a parallel read to Santiago's previously mentioned *21: The Story of Roberto Clemente*. Just as with Clemente's story, sports plays a central role in the overall narrative within the larger context of civil rights.

Yang, G. L. (2013). *Boxers and saints.* New York, NY: First Second Books.

Abstract: This two-volume graphic novel by Gene Luen Yang tells the parallel stories of a Chinese peasant rebelling against Western missionaries and of a young Chinese girl caught in the midst of the Boxer Rebellion.

Chapter 4

Criminal History

Introduction

One of the strongest selling areas among the nonfiction genre is the real crime, or true crime, title. Authors such as Joe MacDonald, Anne Rule, and Dominic Dunne are just as common in book talks as John Grisham, Stephen King, and others. There is a visceral fascination with crime and criminals that easily grips most individuals. It is difficult to pinpoint whether our fascination with crime derives from a particular disgust with the heinous acts, or a bizarre curiosity about the psychological motivations that prompt them. Yet, just as architecture and art can bridge past historical eras and ours, so too can criminals, their acts, and the legal systems that prosecuted them.

Of course, there are some inherent challenges both inside and outside of the classroom when implementing this unique instructional approach. The very nature of the subject matter can create a tense environment depending on the relationship the teacher has established with his or her different administrators and the parents of the students. However, just as with the majority of curriculum and instructional methods, good communication between all parties involved goes a long way in mitigating most difficulties. One of the best ways of facilitating open dialogue and discussion is at the beginning of the academic year, first through a class or course syllabus. Before disseminating the information to the students and parents, conferencing with the campus and district administrators is highly recommended. Establishing a framework and agreeing upon the details with the campus administration before putting together the syllabus and offering it to the students and their parents is a powerful means of establishing a professional relationship that can help if any unforeseen difficulties arise further into the school year.

Regardless of the initial approach by the classroom teacher, crime and criminals are potent and kinetic ways to engage students and challenge them to think both critically and creatively. This approach serves as a means for looking at a particular society in a specific historical era to understand its perspective of what constituted crime and how criminals were treated. In essence, crimes and criminals serve as artifacts for the students and teachers studying that particular time, people, and place. These become de facto guides for the students and teacher, affording a unique point of view. Unlike a course dedicated solely to criminal or legal history, implanting this instructional approach allows these individuals and acts to lead to a hermeneutical construction of context. The severity and illegality of the criminal act can then serve as a beacon for understanding the time and place being explored and investigated by the students. Under the supervision and with the guidance of the teacher, crimes and criminals evolve into emissaries from a different time and place. Through their acts, testimonies, and stories, they speak as much as a work of art or important document does.

Criminal History in the Classroom

The key to engaging students successfully with this particular instructional approach is utilizing narrative devices as a hook or starter to each lesson and to the unit as a whole. However, it is recommended that this instructional method not be used in isolation, but incorporated seamlessly within the regular cycle of instruction. In order to do this, the chronology of the curriculum must drive the instruction. Simply put, whatever historical era, geographic location, and cultural venue are currently being explored should guide the selection of crimes and criminals that are to be studied. In other words, the Code of Hammurabi should not necessarily be investigated while studying Westward Expansion. Of course, if the students have already studied and are familiar with the Code of Hammurabi, then under the guidance of the classroom teacher, the students can be afforded the opportunity to make their own historical and cultural connections.

After a direct teaching of the historical and cultural milieu being studied, the stage is set for an investigation of a true, contextual crime to add depth and complexity to the era. In a certain sense, the study of the crime and the individuals involved plays out like a historical drama. In fact, this metaphor is apt in getting both the classroom teacher and the students to better understand the importance of this type of historical inquiry. Doing this allows the events to unfold kinetically and the characters to develop authentically. This engages the students at a visceral level without sacrificing authenticity.

> ➤ Preteach background information.

> ➤ Divide students into three groups that will be the prosecution, defense, and the jury.

> ➤ Teach students rudiments of trial procedures and legal research.

> ➤ Have students try the case in front of the jury.

> ➤ After the students try and rule on the case, discuss how the case was an exemplar of the time and situation.

FIGURE 4.1. Sample framework.

For this approach, the classroom teacher plays a more prominent role in the daily lesson cycle than with other instructional approaches in this book. Ostensibly, the classroom teacher plays the role of the narrator, both driving and guiding the plot. The challenge facing the teacher is to maintain a delicate balance between instructor and voice of the story. As with any instructional approach, the more a classroom teacher implements it, the more they will become comfortable with the approach and modify and adapt as necessary for the students to get the most out of the experience.

One of the more attractive facets of this unique instructional approach is the challenge it presents to all individuals involved with the educational experience. For both the student and the classroom teacher, the very nature of this instructional investigation challenges everyone to think creatively and critically. Having to approach history with some sense of theater takes a great deal of critical thinking. Once an understanding that the individuals involved in the narrative are actual human beings who lived and died is established, then the instructional approach becomes limitless. This creates an atmosphere in which history truly is living and organic rather than two-dimensional and rote, as is often the case when teaching straight from a textbook.

In the classroom, the students will perform a mock trial as one of the professional products. In doing so, the teacher will need to be somewhat familiar with courtroom procedures. Watching some of the more popular movies or television shows centered on the courtroom can supply more than enough experience in courtroom procedure. If further research is desired, legal reading in both the nonfiction and fiction genres will suffice. Figure 4.1 is a fluid framework and is meant to serve more as an outline rather than as a recipe to be strictly followed.

Before investigating a historical era and a particular culture, the classroom teacher needs to ensure that the students have at least a working knowledge of the time, people, and locations that are the vital setting for the crime and criminals. Something akin to a more traditional social studies approach, such as direct teaching, can easily fulfill this foundational requirement. With the criminal(s) and their acts serving as exemplars of their era and culture, certain precautions must be observed, including:

❖ the nature of the criminal act,
❖ the geographic proximity of the act and individual, and
❖ the historical proximity of the act.

Utilizing this particular instructional approach in the middle school or high school social studies classroom opens up the field and topics of discussion to seemingly innumerable and expansive prospects. In more advanced discussions, the question of ethics and morals is bound to arise. Given the litigious atmosphere that currently resides among the field of public education, some care must be taken by the classroom teacher. Perhaps the best measure to give these discussions legally is also the best means of differentiating in the classroom as teachable moments arise through happenstance. Should these topics arise during the course of investigation, allow the students to generate and explore through discussion. As the classroom teacher, serve as a guide and referee.

Classroom Activity

For the classroom teacher, introducing this particular learning module can resemble something like a police briefing or opening statements made at a criminal trial. When used in my classroom, the implementation provided an excellent opportunity to reach out to some resources available on campus. In this case, the campus School Resource Officer (SRO) was just such a resource. Who better to teach the process of working a criminal arrest and investigation than a uniformed police officer?

Instead of piecing together parts of legal and criminal justice processes, it is a wiser use of time and resources to defer to the local expert. This was a boon in the classroom. It was a perfect chance for the students to see the SRO's expertise. The SRO provided insight to certain criminal justice procedures and processes. The discussion also opened the students' perspective to what the job of a metropolitan police officer is. It was a wonderful experience for all involved, and I hated having to end the class to release the students to their other teachers.

The basic facts of the crime and the individuals involved should be shared with the students. Just enough information about the crime needs to be given to the students in order to ignite their curiosity and inspire their imaginations. This first delving into the world of historical crime should end with predictions and questions from the students regarding the act and the individuals in the form of a flextime summary.

The following class periods are to be filled with student investigations. Evidence, statements, and other facts are to be explored by the students with the ultimate goal not being to establish either guilt or innocence, but to link the criminals and their acts to the historical milieu in which they occurred. This provides an excellent opportunity for students to research, analyze information, and gather information from primary and secondary sources.

Although these are actual acts and individuals, the classroom teacher should challenge the students to think not only critically and creatively, but abstractly. Analyzing these individuals and the acts as symbols of their time, culture, and location challenges students to truly deconstruct and evaluate each component in order to create a final synthesis of their understanding.

Just as important as communicating their understanding of the time, place, and society that bore witness to these criminals' acts and individuals, is to stress the acceptances and celebrate the necessity of lingering questions that will continue to haunt these cases for the foreseeable future. One of the challenges for students in synthesizing their research for this instructional approach is understanding it from multiple points of view. To begin with, the students must analyze the court cases and crimes within the context of the time and places where they occurred. This includes researching the treatment of different ethnicities, genders, and socioeconomic classes. Then, the students must pull back and analyze the situation from a current perspective.

One aspect the classroom teacher must structure a little more is guiding students to an acceptance that some questions will possibly never be answered. Trying to understand why an individual commits a crime is sometimes unanswerable. These unanswered questions not only help the students grow in their thinking processes, but also mature in their appreciation of the complexity of the human condition. To take the point even further, the classroom teacher can challenge the students' level and ability of critical analysis by using the unanswered questions as more than mere tokens of exploration, but also as insight into the uniqueness of our own time, place, and culture, as well as the timelessness of certain aspects of humanity.

Student Products

The capstone product for this instructional method should be one that is both cumulative and formative. Students should be able to communicate their understanding of the era, location, and culture through the aspect of the criminals and the crimes studied. A certain amount of historical and cultural analysis is to be expected. This portion must comprise at least half of the total product. However, the formative aspect is just as valuable for both the students and the teacher involved. This portion needs to be a reflective summary, even a commentary on the learning process and perspective. A summative reflection can be just as powerful and lasting for the students as an evaluative analysis of the content material. Handout 4.1 offers several suggestions for student products.

Examples of professional-level products can be writing a legal brief, making a video presentation, or writing and performing a dramatic monologue as someone involved in the trial. What the classroom teacher needs to ensure is that the students do not settle on just writing a research report, generating a tri-fold display board, or creating a PowerPoint presentation. These three venues have been overdone. By the time students have made it to the secondary level, they have mastered these three products. Part of these instructional activities is to expose and offer students opportunities that they will encounter in the professional realm.

Assessment

The best way to approach measuring student achievement with this particular instructional approach is utilizing rubrics. The general rubric provided in the appendix can be easily adapted to assess the many products that can be used with this chapter.

Handout 4.1
Criminal History

Select a piece of criminal history from a particular region/era/culture and analyze it using the following two-step process:

Step 1

Examine the piece of criminal history and see if you can fully answer the following questions:

- ❖ What does this piece tell you about the people?
- ❖ What does it tell you about the historical era?
- ❖ What does it tell you about the geographic location and place?
- ❖ How does it serve as an example to explain this particular culture/society in this time and place?

Step 2

Using the answers and understanding from Step 1, select one of the three options to complete the analysis of the criminal history/crime:

Option 1: Reanalyze the piece of criminal history/crime in modern times in order to reflect the time, place, and culture in which you live.

Option 2: Examine a different piece of criminal history/crime from the same time, place, and culture that the original piece originated from. Write an extended research paper analyzing the crime and its full historical context.

Option 3: Create an original piece of criminal history/crime from a completely new and unique civilization that you have created.

Format(s)

When completing Step 2 of the analysis, you are only limited by your imagination in completing the piece. Some more popular formats include: graphic novels, comic strips, videos, dramatic monologues, as well as others . . . *Go forth and create!*

Annotated Bibliography

Baatz, S. (2009). *For the thrill of it: Leopold, Loeb, and the murder that shocked Jazz Age Chicago*. New York, NY: Harper Perennial.

Abstract: This particular text by Simon Baatz examines the murder of a child committed in 1924 by Nathan Leopold and Richard Loeb. These two eventually confessed to killing for the thrill of it. Looking at how the crime and subsequent confession shaped the nation's conscience will help students see the significance of crime in studying history.

Larson, E. (2004). *The devil in the white city: Murder, magic, and madness at the fair that changed America*. New York, NY: Vintage.

Abstract: Erik Larson's insightful and invigorating work surrounds America's first serial killer and the Columbian Exposition in 1893. This well-researched and readable book is a treat for students and their teachers alike.

Lieberman, P. (2012). *Gangster squad: Covert cops, the mob, and the battle for Los Angeles*. New York, NY: St. Martin's Press.

Abstract: Paul Lieberman's telegraphic writing style rattles off the thrilling true story of the battle between the Los Angeles Police Department and the mob for control of the city after World War II. Sharing this adventure with students so they can understand how this fight shaped an age and a city is a powerful teaching tool.

Chapter 5

Culinary History

Introduction

Cooking, eating, gardening, and other culinary acts are deeply ingrained within our DNA. Even individuals who cannot or refuse to cook for themselves can enjoy a tasty meal and a memorable experience that engages almost all of the senses. In fact, this is one of the reasons why eating and cooking are such sought-after pastimes. This and the ease and affordability make it an attractive solitary or collective undertaking. So much of our communication and community has been built on or around cooking and eating. Only recently has the historical study of culinary practices become a serious academic undertaking in understanding the nuances of culture and shades of history. However, this approach to historical and anthropological study is somewhat relegated to professional practitioners and academics. Yet, this approach to learning and teaching what is a major component of social studies is ripe for use in the middle school classroom.

Implementing an interdisciplinary educational experience such as this will not only ignite the natural excitement of adolescents in exploring something new, but also reinvigorate the intellectual curiosity that seems to have diminished in the majority of students by the time they have matriculated to middle school. Also, this is one of the few classroom educational experiences that allow the students to literally get dirty, make a mess, and learn from it. This instructional method allows for authentic assessment and peer critique almost immediately. Utilizing food and culinary arts within the core content classroom also allows students to explore possible professional opportunities within a safe environment that encourages experimentation and exploration.

Culinary History in the Classroom

Implementing this particular instructional approach in the social studies classroom lies within two realms, the academic and the experiential. It is recommended that the classroom teacher who wishes to implement this unique approach prepare with some research prior to the beginning of the school year. The reason for this is that utilizing the study of food and the culinary arts to enhance and guide the instruction of social studies content can potentially span the entirety of the academic year.

Due to the increased popular interest in this subject and the numerous activities that have sprung up surrounding food and culinary arts, finding resources is not as difficult as it once was. The explosion of cooking channels, books, and magazines attest to more than just the mere trendiness of the topic. However, food preparation and celebration can be as foreign a concept as another language for many middle school students. In fact, approaching this particular instructional method as if it were a totally foreign language may the best means of welcoming students into this study. Doing such will also help to welcome students who may truly be unfamiliar with this concept and learning environment. It may even promote learning outside of the classroom (the eternal hope of most all educators) and encourage students to explore their own culinary topography.

If the curriculum scope and sequence allows for it, one of the approaches that is highly recommended for the classroom teacher is to have students investigate and create their own culinary personality (i.e., what kind of foods and flavors they like). This already places the level of rigor well at the top of Bloom's taxonomy. The creation and exploration of their own individual personalities will help students internalize the learning and further ignite their curiosity. This is the ultimate goal of all classroom teachers regardless of grade level or content area.

From a holistic perspective, especially one that is familiar to teachers with professional annual evaluations, this classroom approach is a vibrant mixture of individual, group, and teacher-led investigations and analyses. It is a means of capitalizing on heavily researched best practices while hitting all of the primary domains on the majority of teacher evaluations. But more importantly, igniting the students' curiosity and imagination is the ultimate goal.

The recommended span of this lesson cycle is 1–2 school weeks. Integrated into this lesson cycle, and the teacher's discretion, is foundational knowledge of the time, location, and culture reflected by the food and its ingredients. From experience, it is best if the few class periods prior to investigating a culinary culture are spent building a foundational knowledge

As with the majority of the other classroom approaches explored in this book, a knowledge bank can be obtained through regular textbooks along with simple web searches. This type of familiarity is essential for students to not only make connections, but to ask the probing questions that form the basis of authentic learning.

At the beginning of this unit, it is recommended that the social studies teacher collaborate with the English/language arts and science teachers in order to fully address the topic. Analyzing the literature surrounding culinary arts is an essential way to open the story of food and culture to students who may not have necessarily traveled anywhere outside of their immediate locale. Although food writing, such as restaurant reviews, is immediately approachable and very reader friendly, it is also subjective and personal.

One genre of food literature that is perennially overlooked for study is recipes. These written pieces are an art form within themselves. In fact, approaching a recipe as one would approach a piece of poetry definitely opens up the discussion to a higher level of analysis. One of the more powerful aspects of implementing this is the no-fault approach to interpretation and analysis. What this means is simply that there are no wrong answers, for the most part, when it comes to the students' interpretation. Reading recipes as poetry rather than just as steps to follow or instructions can challenge students. Reading a recipe with all of the senses immediately evokes an equally sensory response. Affording students the challenge and chance to creatively respond to either a single recipe or a set of selected recipes transitions critical thinking to higher levels.

Science comes into play as well in this instructional approach. This is particularly true with regard to ingredients, measurements, and changes that occur during the preparation of food. Looking at the ingredients as signs and symbols of the location that not only produced them, but incorporated them into local dishes allows these to evolve into primary sources speaking to current students across time and distance. As the trend of cooking local produce—individuals who practice this have been nicknamed locavores—continues to gain strength, it cannot be ignored. It is a perfect means of incorporating this classroom instructional approach while also compiling a working knowledge of the local community with the students.

Classroom Activity

Implementing this instructional approach is actually not much different than teaching a historical period, graphic location, or specific culture using music. Once the fundamental knowledge has been attained by the students, it is time to introduce the ingredients, recipes, and finished culinary products. In fact, each of these components should be introduced and implemented in that order. It is time to let the food begin speaking for itself. Creating a culinary dish from established recipes with the students draws their natural curiosity and innate interest. It opens up social studies- and science-based discussions about sustainability and a consciousness of place, moves the exploration to a global stage for the students, and challenges them to engage the topic in a way that allows them to constructively add to the discussion.

Once the backstory of the culture, history, and location of a recipe or dish has been established and explored, the ingredients become something akin to the chorus in a classical Greek drama. Giving the story behind the spices allows them to become characters in the exploration and investigation itself. However, the probing should not end at this particular point of the lesson cycle. Entire dishes and complete menus are the next stop. As such, the foods and meals need to be placed within the hermeneutical context being studied at that time.

This approach allows history, geography, and even science to come alive and interact with the students in a visceral and vibrant manner. Not only will this approach make the subject literally come alive in the classroom, but may also open up the possibilities of further studying culinary arts for secondary students.

Student Product

With the completion of the introductory and foundational implements completed, the educational experience now turns to application according to Bloom's taxonomy. If the campus allows and has the necessary equipment, it is time to beginning cooking for and ultimately cooking with your students. Certain safeguards and precautions must be established and implemented in doing this. If the school campus does not have an operable kitchen allowing the students to work and learn, then a regular science laboratory set-up will suffice. Students can choose to make a simple dish from a particular region of the world or a particular historical era. Handout 5.1 offers some more suggestions for student products.

Assessment

Needless to say, assessment should not be based on how good or bad the students' dishes taste. Instead, adapt the general rubric that's provided in the appendix to assess how well the students were able to connect history and geography to the dishes they made.

Handout 5.1
Tasting History

Select a piece of culinary arts from a particular region/era/culture and analyze using the following two step process:

Step 1

Examine the piece of culinary arts and see if you can fully answer the following questions:

- ❖ What does this piece tells you about the people who created it?
- ❖ What does it tell you about the time in which it was created?
- ❖ What does it tell you about the place where it was created?
- ❖ How does it serve as an example to explain this particular culture/society in this time and place?

Step 2

Using the answers and understanding from Step 1, select one of the three options to complete the analysis of the culinary arts:

Option 1: Recreate the piece of culinary arts in modern times in order to reflect the time, place, and culture in which you live, so that it is able to answer the same questions from Step 1.

Option 2: Create an original piece of culinary arts from the same time, place, and culture that the original piece originated from, one that is able to answer the same questions from Step 1.

Option 3: Create an original piece of culinary arts from a completely new and unique civilization that you have created. This piece of culinary art must be able to fully answer the questions from Step 1.

Format(s)

When completing Step 2 of the analysis, you are only limited by your imagination in completing the piece. Some more popular formats include: recipes, cooking demonstrations, videos, dramatic monologues, as well as others . . . *Go forth and create!*

Annotated Bibliography

Clark, E. (2006). *The oysters of Loqmariaquer*. New York, NY: Harper Perennial.

Abstract: Eleanor Clark's classic gastronomic literature from the first half of the 20th century focuses on a single food source found in a single region of France. The author wholly exemplifies the objectives in this instructional approach. A great pairing may be even preparing some of the dishes explored in the book.

Kurlansky, M. (1998). *Cod: A biography of the fish that changed the world*. New York, NY: Penguin.

Abstract: This work by Mark Kurlansky challenges the reader to consider the pivotal role this simple fish has played in building Atlantic civilization since medieval times, if not earlier. Utilizing this book will help students better understand the role of food and cooking in the greater historical narrative.

Kurlansky, M. (2003). *Salt: A world history*. New York, NY: Penguin.

Abstract: In this book, Mark Kurlansky interweaves culinary history with geography, politics, religion, and culture. The resulting dish is as savory and tangy as the spice named in the title. The gripping narrative reads more like an adventure story than culinary history.

Chapter 6

Science History

Introduction

One of the burgeoning subfields in history that has gleaned greater popular and scholarly support recently is that of scientific and medical history. These unique disciplines and areas of academic inquiry have quickly made their way into the popular consciousness of the reading public. In fact, Siddhartha Mukherjee won the 2011 Pulitzer Prize for his foundational work *The Emperor of All Maladies*, which chronicled the cultural and scientific history of cancer from the earliest known cases recorded by ancient Greek physicians. Even though Mukherjee is a practicing oncologist and research scientist, his prose and style invites the layman into the labyrinthine timeline of cancer's historical narrative. This novel-like story is entrancing and just what is needed in the secondary social studies classroom to engage and excite students. Including scientific and medical history is an effective means of igniting the latent curiosity and inquisitiveness of adolescent learners.

The atmosphere is ripe for science classroom teachers to utilize this wave of popularity with novel classroom instruction. Try implementing popular science books, video clips, and student-generated music and documentaries based on core content knowledge. This instructional approach popularizes and reinvigorates the tired and worn-out means of teaching social studies that have lingered in some classrooms for far too long. This classroom perspective also affords the teacher the opportunity to teach well outside of his or her regularly expected boundaries that students have grown accustomed to over time. It also challenges students to think more critically and creatively from a global and holistic perspective.

Science History in the Classroom

This approach guides the students in making essential connections and discovering the relevance of the knowledge and skills in a self-directed manner as analysis becomes more evident to the individual students. Incorporating the curious and unique combination of the abstract and concrete that comprises science with the seemingly rote nature of social studies, students are able to actually touch pieces of history. Retracing some of the explorations and experiments that were novel and cutting edge at the time the scientists made them provides students with a chance to experience the science in historical context. These experiences open doorways that will help guide the students in deep to what they may at first consider to be some mundane facts. It is far more effective than just lecturing or having the students copy down a timeline of science.

Also, this approach helps add a particular level of rigor to the instruction by broadening the scope to include another subject area or two. Interestingly, science is one of the subject areas at the secondary level that is one of the more difficult to teach due to the abstract nature of the material. Teaching middle school students about the nature and composition of an atom, balancing chemical equations, or about Newton's Three Laws can truly be a challenge when the majority of students are either still operating at or transitioning from the concrete operational level of cognition. Adding the human backstory to create context with the content and/or skill gives the students the ability to bridge from the concrete to the abstract a little more easily.

What kinds of narratives should be employed in this particular implementation is the next relevant question to arise. The narratives should be the stories of the accidents, adventures, and inventions that that resulted in astounding scientific discoveries. There are numerous approachable popular science texts. I've listed my recommendations in the annotated bibliography at the end of the chapter. These struggles, triumphs, and tragedies add color and depth to the study of both science and social studies. They humanize the study of science, removing it from the impersonal, sterile laboratory environment.

But the recurring question is, "Why science?" This is perhaps one of, if not the, most feared content areas by social studies teachers at the secondary level. It is an indispensable subject for students to not only learn, but to ultimately appreciate, as much of its historical narrative as possible. This portion of history, once neglected, has been recently explored both by historians and scientists in order to better understand how far science has advanced and where it may go.

Once the question of *why* has been addressed, the question of *how* comes to the forefront. As with some of the other instructional methods explored in the book, this one does require some preplanning and preparation by the classroom teacher prior to implementing it. However, the preparation is actually much easier than the majority of classroom teachers may think at first.

The majority of the preparation for implementation on the part of the classroom teacher is simply reading. Of course, what to read and how is part of the challenge facing the teachers as well. One of the best means of locating titles is simply searching the Internet for books under the heading "science writing" and "science journalism." Many of the popular science titles are also located on national bestseller lists and book reviews. Looking at sites for retailers such as Barnes & Noble, Amazon, and others will also expand the list of titles available. Local and campus libraries are a virtually untapped resource often overlooked or ignored.

There are a number of popular science communicators, such as Brian Greene, Neil Degrasse Tyson, Jane Goodall, Craig Childs, and others. Some universities such as Columbia, M.I.T., and Berkeley offer courses and degrees in science journalism and science writing. The websites for these schools and their programs are also a good starting point to gather names and titles to begin building a science library.

One of the better metaphors in understanding the responsibilities of the classroom teacher with this implementation is that of the college professor. Unlike the educators in the K–12 spectrum, college professors usually teach from a variety of sources, very few of them being textbooks. As such, reading with the goal of teaching in mind challenges the teacher to read for a different level of comprehension than reading for pleasure or understanding. In essence, these books and articles need to be read with a pencil in hand and a good understanding of the curriculum standards.

One of the perks of this is that the teacher does not necessarily have to read the entirety of the selected texts. The primary goal of the reading is locating and recording anecdotes surrounding the particular historical individuals, events, and discoveries. These stories will help the students appreciate the person, the time, and his or her accomplishments within the context of the social studies classroom.

Classroom Activity

Incorporating stories such as these facilitates a rapport between the teacher and students. It also sets the classroom teacher in the position of storyteller and the students as the audience. Although studies show a dramatic decrease in student retention when direct teaching through lecturing occurs, this is something completely different. In this practice, students will retain more information with the vehicle of oral storytelling in place. Cultivating a rich storytelling environment for students in the secondary classroom may actually result in gaining a greater share of the students' attention rather than having to constantly battle to direct it. It is a simple act of capitalizing on the direction in which communication and language are moving rather than clutching to tired old methods.

Figure 6.1 offers a sample time frame and activities to implement this approach. This framework can be expanded or contracted as needed or dictated by the curriculum scope and sequence along with the individual teacher's pacing. An understanding of the context is necessary to cultivate a true appreciation of the individuals, inventions, and discoveries to be experienced.

Student Products

The final student products can vary, in both rigor and creativity, according to the teacher's resources and needs. Students can write a research paper on a historical scientific innovation, or they can perform a dramatic interpretation of the scientists and circumstances that led to that innovation. The only limit to this is imagination, but it's important that whatever they produce, the students capture the human story and historical import behind the scientific discovery they're reporting on. Handout 6.1 mentions some suggestions for student products.

Assessment

Overall, the objective of this instructional approach is to guide the students in making independent connections between scientists, their discoveries and/or inventions, and the historical and geographical context being studied. Doing this personalizes and humanizes the content of social studies in a way that makes it not only more accessible to the student, but also more real in regards to the successes and failures of these individuals. It also goes far in opening the science curriculum up to the students and assisting them in making the cross-curricular connections with the content knowledge. Teachers should think of these things when using the general rubric (provided in the appendix) to assess student products.

➢ The first class period of this approach focuses on bridging the known context of the time, location, and events already understood by the students with the new information that the teacher will supply through an oral narrative.

  o During this learning session, the teacher can guide the discussion in order to establish connections between scientific knowledge and social studies information. The primary objective of this class period is for the students to understand the scientist(s) and/or their inventions and discoveries as exemplars of their particular time and possibly location.

  o As an ending activity, the classroom teacher can have the students reiterate the connection made by the teacher in the narrative shared during the lesson. This can be done with a short, written reflection or summary on a blank 3" x 5" card and used as a "ticket" out the door for dismissal.

➢ The opening of the second class period can be used to refresh the students' memory of the prior class period in order to prepare them for the next activity, which is completed with a fellow student under the guidance of the classroom teacher. This can be used as the warm up to the class activity. After completing the warm-up and discussing it, have students work with a partner to bridge an assigned scientist and discovery with the historical era and geographic location. Students should have available to them not only their notes, textbooks, and other classroom materials, but also research materials often found in the library, especially computers. This is an opportune time to support research techniques, especially which sites and sources are to be used and proper citation. The primary questions driving this particular exercise are as follows:

  o How does the scientist relate and represent the historical era that they lived in?

  o How does the discovery/invention fit within the era it was made?

  o In what way does the individual and his or her discovery/invention serve as representatives of his or her time and location?

  o How did this individual and his or her discovery/invention add to the ongoing story of history and science?

➢ When the students have completed and compiled their research, the teacher can direct them to presenting their research in a product. This can be anything from an information card to a poster to a dramatic monologue. Each pair of students must present their findings in a manner that effectively engages their peers. By the end of the second class period, the students should have their product ready to present.

FIGURE 6.1. Sample timeframe and activities.

o The third class session is entirely devoted to the presentation of information. Peers should—with the teacher's guidance—question, evaluate, and comment on their presentation and on the knowledge of the presenters. The end of the period needs to be centered on the overall experience in preparation for the upcoming sessions.

o The following two class periods are set aside for individual research and production. The classroom teacher makes available a list of scientists and their discoveries or inventions for the students to select from. These are the topics that the students will research and present on after 2 days of research and preparation. The final day (possibly 2 days depending on the size of the class) is given to the students' presentation of their products and their peer critiques.

o The format for the last three class periods are structured similarly to the previous two except that this final research project is done individually and with less guidance from the classroom teacher.

  • The students' projects are different than the products discussed in previous chapters. For this instructional approach, the students will be presenting a more professional talk, discussion, or presentation. The finished product is more traditional than the ones suggested in the earlier chapters.

FIGURE 6.1. Continued.

Handout 6.1
Scientific History

Select a scientific discovery or invention from a particular region/era/culture and analyze it using the following two-step process:

Step 1

Examine the discovery or invention and see if you can fully answer the following questions:

❖ What does this piece tell you about the people who discovered/created it?
❖ What does it tell you about the time in which it was discovered/created?
❖ What does it tell you about the place where it was discovered/created?
❖ How does it serve as an example to explain this particular culture/society in this time and place?

Step 2

Using the answers and understanding from Step 1, select one of the three options to complete the analysis of the scientific discovery or invention:

Option 1: Recreate the scientific discovery or invention in modern times in order to reflect the time, place, and culture in which you live.

Option 2: Examine another scientific discovery or invention from the same time, place, and culture that the original piece originated from.

Option 3: Generate an original scientific discovery or invention from a completely new and unique civilization that you have created.

Format(s)

When completing Step 2 of the analysis, you are only limited by your imagination in completing the piece. Some more popular formats include: graphic novels, comic strips, videos, dramatic monologues, as well as others . . . ***Go forth and create!***

Note: The presentation of these products should be on a professional level and be somewhat more formal than most other products in this text.

Annotated Bibliography

Blum, D. (2011). *The poisoner's handbook: Murder and the birth of forensic medicine in Jazz Age New York*. New York, NY: Penguin.

Abstract: This book by Deborah Blum chronicles the birth of forensic medicine against the backdrop of Jazz Age corruption in the New York City coroner's office. This text will guide students though the evolution of modern chemistry and medicine as well as forensic science. They can see how what was once thought healthy is now known as poisonous.

Essig, M. (2009). *Edison and the electric chair: A story of light and death*. London, England: Walker.

Abstract: Mark Essig unveils the shrouded and convoluted history behind what was supposed to be a more humane means of capital punishment. This text offers an excellent examination of history, science, culture, law, as well as law enforcement. Students will gain a better understanding of the uses and misunderstandings of science.

Jonnes, J. (2010). *Eiffel's tower: The thrilling story behind Paris's beloved monument and the extraordinary world's fair that produced it*. New York, NY: Penguin.

Abstract: With this work, Jill Jonnes firmly places the creation and construction of the Eiffel Tower well within its proper historical and cultural context. Incorporating this text with this instructional approach not only supports the objectives, but offers the students a readable narrative that will expand their understanding.

Chapter 7

Forgotten History

Introduction

One of the sad facts of social studies education is that even with block or regular scheduling, 187 class days is nowhere near enough time to cover even the essentials in most subjects. Many times the depth and complexity of what some may consider "supporting characters" in history and culture are left unstudied. However, even with the hyperfocus on standardized testing and measured student achievement, there is a way to "sneak" in these silent voices into the social studies classroom and ignite the interests of the students, some of whom may have been wholly disinterested before learning of and hearing from these individuals.

Two of the more left-out or ignored groups of individuals in history are women and what are traditionally labeled as minorities. Although history at the collegiate level has opened up more to include the voices and stories of these two important groups, at the middle and high school levels, progress is grindingly slow. State standards are just now beginning to list suggested names of previously absent individuals from these two groups. This particular instructional method is an effective and engaging way of igniting students' latent curiosity through broadening the overall narrative of social studies to include the previously silent voices.

Forgotten History in the Classroom

At this point, the burning question is how and where to begin this approach. Like many of the techniques explored in this text, there is a certain degree of front-loading on the part of the classroom teacher. He or she can parallel read the primary sources with the students, but prior preparation is always recommended. At the end of the chapter, an annotated bibliography of suggested works to use when implementing this specific classroom instructional strategy is provided.

Primary sources, which serve as a major foundational facet of social studies, are the keystones to implementing this strategy. Given the increased amount of digitized primary sources, most of which are offered free of charge, the access for the classroom teacher is readily available. This will assist the teacher in preparing and implementing the activity. Primary sources cover everything from letters to songs to works of art. For this particular method, the pieces used will focus on written and pictorial genres. This leaves a vast panorama available for students to explore and investigate. These primary sources will allow the voices from the period being studied to speak directly to the students through the pieces examined. The classroom teacher needs to be thoroughly acquainted with the primary source pieces prior to exposing the students to them through a class activity.

One way of understanding the nature and workings of the classroom is to utilize the metaphor of the theater. The teacher must juggle numerous roles and responsibilities. For our intents and purposes in this chapter, the teacher must play the lead role of the author or artist of the primary source. He or she is responsible for bringing to life two-dimensional written and painted pieces to express their innate depth and complexity, which may be missed if left up to individual student exploration. The classroom teacher enables the students to witness the events and era through the experiences and perspective of the person or groups in richer detail than a textbook or film can give.

Many of the traditionally marginalized students—females, students of color, and students from low-socioeconomic backgrounds—have responded eagerly to hearing and reading about individuals in history that have come from groups and situations similar to theirs. This simple instructional setting allows the students the opportunity to establish and cultivate a lasting connection with history through a means that will assist the students in maintaining the historical knowledge as long-term memory. It may also give the students a very personal sense of history and belonging.

For students who may fall within these populations, this is an excellent opportunity to explore and navigate new and different territory than what they may be accustomed to or familiar with. Gentle guidance and compassionate questioning of all students involved by the teacher is not only the best classroom practice, but also a strong example of the best of humanity that anyone can give to another person. In fact, given the perilous condition that social studies education, and by default humanities and civics education, are currently in, a strong display of humanity may be just the proverbial shot in the arm that is need at this time.

Although the reasoning behind implementing this particular approach in the classroom is evident, what it looks like, how to implement it, and how to assess its efficacy among a wide population of students still remains to be explored. The example framework laid out in the following pages will correspond to a regular 5-day school week. Each of the class periods will refer to an approximate 53-minute block of time. These are merely guidelines. The classroom teachers choosing to implement this method will need to adapt and improvise according to their set schedule and audience of students from class to class. It is important that the teacher have a firm grasp as to the overall character and personality of their classes, and that the classes have had prior exposure to and experience working with primary sources before encountering these particular pieces from lesser known sources. In fact, having had prior experience with primary sources from more known individuals will help to place these newer pieces in proper perspective and context.

Classroom Activity

The student, under the guidance of the teacher, will establish the space and place where a new voice can reside within the overall historical, geographical, and cultural narrative. As with any instructional method, especially one that is new, some prior planning and foundational work must be done in order to prepare the students for the challenges they will face in the upcoming activities A working knowledge of the time period, geographic location, particular place, and culture(s) inhabiting it is necessary for the students to fully appreciate and investigate the primary sources presented to them. This can be included in the first class period of the instructional activity.

One of the recommended means of presenting this foundational information to the students is through a computer presentation, an outlined discussion, or a paired activity based on a scavenger hunt followed by a direct teach to ensure correct and complete information. Regardless, the classroom teacher will be the best judge of which method and pace is appropriate given the learning styles and processing of his or her individual students. It is essential that the students have a base level of understanding of the context of the primary sources in order to properly place them within the correct milieu for investigation and examination. Once the classroom teacher has attained mastery of the foundational knowledge from the students, the class can move on to the second part of the activity.

Once the students can better understand the actual time and place where the primary sources originated from, it is time to immerse the students in the sources themselves. In doing so, these selected piece(s) evolve into more than what they are, or appear to be. They are no longer letters, journal entries, editorials, or speeches. With a true immersion, these primary sources become an extension of the time, place, and individual who created and composed them. They bridge the distances time and geography have created. The second part of the investigation turns the table on the classroom activity. It is time for the students to lead their own exploration and give voice to the individuals following the pattern the classroom teacher established in the earlier part of the lesson cycle, but not too closely.

Presenting students with primary sources such as newspaper stories, criminal records, and court transcripts opens a treasure chest for the students. However, the classroom teacher needs to be comfortable working with primary sources. Guiding students through a classroom conversation with these sources, the teacher can introduce students to these forgotten voices. Also, the teacher can open up a dialogue between the students and the sources.

Student Products

Once the students have been afforded the opportunity to explore their primary sources, then they can begin to adapt themselves to being the voice of the individual who composed and created the primary source. Just as the classroom teacher brought the particular primary source to life to the whole class through a dramatic reading, the individual students will be tasked with something similar with their selected or assigned primary sources.

It is recommended that the students use primarily text-based sources, which will be easiest to adapt into dramatic monologues. If students desire to move into more visual sources, it is further recommended that they stay within the framework of photographs, paintings, and posters. Utilizing visual primary sources like television shows or films may keep the students from connecting deeply and personally with the material.

By definition, a dramatic monologue is a written or spoken piece delivered from the single point of view of a character, usually a major one. Similarly, the students can take the first-person narrative from the primary source and turn it into a dramatic narrative suitable for either reading or performing, or both. This makes for a high-level final product that bridges social studies with both ELA and theater arts/drama. However, this does require a high level of discipline regarding research, writing, and eventual staging of the piece. Likewise, it calls for a certain level of oversight and guidance on the part of the classroom teacher. This is to ensure that the proper balance of historical accuracy and artistic flourish is maintained so that one does not trump the other. Should the historical accuracy gain ground over the students' artistry, then the dramatic monologue runs the risk of becoming merely a monologue akin to traditional documentaries with talking heads dominating the scene. On the other hand, should the artistry of the piece hold sway, then the opposite may occur and the monologue may develop into a fully fledged dramatic production without much, if any, historical accuracy. Handout 7.1 offers some guiding questions and suggestions for the student product.

Assessment

In assessing students' dramatic monologues, have them consider it similar to giving a speech with a more dramatic delivery—the student will be taking on the role of a specific individual. The teacher should try to guide students to think equally about the information they are delivering as well as how they are delivering it. Another helpful analogy is to have students approach their monologues as they would if they were preparing for readers' theater activities in the classroom.

Finally, the classroom teacher must be aware of the appropriateness of the material. The students will be quick to pick up on the humanity of their subject, and will be even more ready to share it with their audience. This offers a very teachable moment for self-editing and appropriateness. Grabbing an audience's interest with just enough titillating facts and leaving them wanting more is what good entertainers—and great educators—do on a regular basis. The general rubric provided in the appendix can be easily adapted to fit these criteria.

Handout 7.1

Silent and Forgotten
Voices in History

Select a piece of forgotten or silent history from a particular culture and analyze it using the following two-step process:

Step 1

Examine the piece and see if you can fully answer the following questions:
- ❖ What does this piece tell you about the people who were involved in it?
- ❖ What does it tell you about the time in which it occurred?
- ❖ What does it tell you about the place where it happened?
- ❖ How does it serve as an example to explain this particular culture/society in this time and place?

Step 2

Using the answers and understanding from Step 1, select one of the three options to complete the analysis of the forgotten or silent history:

Option 1: Recreate the piece of forgotten or silent in modern times in order to reflect the time, place, and culture in which you live.

Option 2: Examine a different piece of forgotten or silent history from the same time, place, and culture that the original piece originated from.

Option 3: Create an original piece of forgotten or silent history from a completely new and unique civilization that you have created.

Format(s)

When completing Step 2 of the analysis, you are only limited by your imagination in presenting the piece. Some more popular formats include: videos, dramatic monologues, and others . . . ***Go forth and create!***

Annotated Bibliography

McCourt, F. (1996). *Angela's ashes*. New York, NY: Scribner.

Abstract: Frank McCourt's first volume in his informal trilogy gives a gritty and realistic portrayal of life for the poor in Ireland in the mid-20th century. Few people escape this harsh life and fewer still write about it with such candor and fortitude. As difficult as this content may be, it is a powerful instructional tool.

Moody, A. (1992). *Coming of age in Mississippi*. New York, NY: Dell.

Abstract: This is a powerful, instructive, and enlightening book. No matter what capacity it is used in the classroom, or who reads it, its capacity to change individuals is phenomenal. Whether used as a whole text or in excerpts, Moody's book definitely supports the learning outcomes of this particular unit.

Skloot, R. (2011). *The immortal life of Henrietta Lacks*. New York, NY: Broadway.

Abstract: In this particular true-life detective story, Skloot tells the story of a poor tobacco farmer whose cells went on to make medical history. The only catch is that Lack and her family did not know about any of it, until now. Skloot's book is an exemplar of this unit's learning objectives.

Chapter 8

Local History

Introduction

For teachers, one of the greatest challenges is having enough resources. Many times the resources available are cost prohibitive. Yet, there is one resource for the social studies classroom that is too often overlooked: local history. No matter where we teach and live, we are surrounded by history. Although local history is usually one of the first resources passed over, it can be given its proper due while maintaining the standardized test timeline. Moreover, studying local history is a great way to cover core content areas for social studies while encouraging students to learn about and make connections with their local communities.

Local History in the Classroom

So the major question remains as to what local history is and what its place can be in a secondary-level social studies class. Local history is the starting point, and many times the ending point, of numerous historical investigations. The teacher needs to be vigilant in reminding the students that they are reporting history, not creating it. Given the content the students are learning and producing, local history provides an opportune platform for practicing skills such as researching, writing, interviewing, and even directing and editing a short film. Studying local history also provides an opportunity for the school community of students and teachers to expand and incorporate itself into the larger local community.

What this allows to happen is a discovery, or recovery, of links and ties that may have been forgotten and overlooked for many years or generations. It is the local community that built the physical school buildings and the communal school system. Likewise, many times the faculty and staff come from the community as well. Similarly, the students are members of the larger, external community. But for many students, given their academic stage and age, it is challenging to understand the larger community outside of their immediate classroom. Even within the classroom, it is difficult for them to imagine their community beyond the confines of their immediate friends. This exploration and interaction can help students to explore more of who they are in relation to the community they are living and learning in.

With the ease of access that students have to technology, there is little argument that the world is figuratively growing smaller each day. Yet, with all of this connectivity, one could easily posit that individuals are more disconnected at a local level. Guiding students to burrow deep in their own community, sometimes even into their own families, gives them a greater sense of self than many other extracurricular activities can. It is a unique experience that can dredge up proverbial ghosts and skeletons, but can also give a new generation with a fresh perspective a chance to deal with spotted history and guide the community into the future. If nothing else, studying local history can give the students an opportunity to understand their local community better in order to appreciate their place for what it is, what it was, and what it might come to be.

Delving and diving into local history is an effective means for sparking a genuine interest in not only history as a subject, but history as a verb. But, what does that mean—history as a verb? This is perhaps one of the most longstanding and vexing questions that faces both students and teachers in social studies. Sometimes answering how one *does* or studies history is just as important as what history *is*. Upon first glance, this may come across as more of a philosophical exploration than a practical application, but it actually embodies both. By literally practicing, or *doing*, history, students and teachers can pragmatically determine *what* exactly history *is*. In doing so, with this particular understanding and point of view, students and teachers take ownership of history by carving out their own perspectives, and more importantly, their own shared definition of history, its essence, and its practice.

Once the students and the classroom teacher have a firm grasp of what history is and an understanding of what to expect, it is time to get busy with the activity. Sometimes the best place to begin practicing local history is right within the classroom or on the immediate campus. Many times, the immediate surroundings prove to be just as fertile a field for historical research as any museum, library, or archive. The challenge that presents itself immediately to the teacher is the task of exciting the students to the historical narratives that surround them. This is where the powers of the teacher's abilities as a storyteller come into play. At this crucial point, the teacher's ability to hook the students' attention and interest can either make or break the entire experience. Part of successful and engaging instruction is presentation. And a crucial component of effective presentation is entertainment in order to capture and cultivate the audiences' (i.e., the students') interest.

Classroom Activities

The classroom activity can take many forms. Perhaps the best way to approach it is to guide the students in thinking about making a commercial or mini-documentary about their subject relating to local history. These two tangible, real-world products are ones that students can easily relate to. It also provides an excellent opportunity for the teacher to utilize technology in the classroom.

The campus library is often the most opportune starting point for this particular activity. Previous yearbooks, trophies, newspaper clippings, and other such mementos can be found here; in many ways, the school library often serves as an archive for the entire school. Other locations that may yield similar findings would be the fine and performing arts and athletics departments. These two extracurricular electives frequently preserve their own histories as well as showcase them. It's worth noting that in many schools, staff turnover is relatively infrequent, so conducting oral histories can be very productive for students. Once the students have achieved a partial glimpse of the multidimensional layers in their community, they will begin to understand that they are not only a character in the ongoing narrative, but also responsible for telling part of and carrying on the story. In some schools or districts that multiple generations of families have attended, implementing this particular approach to conducting historical research allows students to explore their own family's historical narrative within the context of the larger community's.

Student Products

As with most any project involving historical research, the primary components of this approach is comprised of the two traditional practices that have populated the work of historians for ages: research and writing. The research may consist of the traditional delving in and navigating through the archives and libraries. In this case, the campus library should do the trick. The other portion of this aspect of the instructional approach is the writing. The classroom teacher implementing this particular instructional approach cannot assume that the students have had any particular experience with historical research and writing. As such, it is paramount that the classroom teacher incorporates lessons focused on historical research and writing within the context of studying local history.

> ➤ Mini-documentary posted on YouTube
>
> ➤ Interactive museum display
>
> ➤ Oral history project
>
> ➤ Recorded interviews
>
> ➤ Multimedia presentation

FIGURE 8.1. Sample products.

When the students have completed their research, it is time for them to generate a professional-level product. As with the other instructional approaches explored in this book, a great amount of latitude and flexibility at this stage is given to the teacher concerning the students' output. As previously mentioned, it is crucial at this stage that classroom teachers authentically gauge the performance and product of the students as a measurement of their individual progress over time within the context of the content-based skills that the students were expected to operate within during the course of the project. Figure 8.1 lists some possible products that students may incorporate with this instructional approach. Handout 8.1 offers some guiding questions and more suggestions for the student product.

Assessment

Building a summative reflection into nearly each and every assignment regardless of its scope and rigor is vital for the overall success of student comprehension and retention. I recommend guiding the students through a reflective summary at the end of this unit with journaling activities and other such assignments. This will allow them to reflect on the connections they made to the local community. Pair a summative reflection with the general rubric to assess the students' products and retention.

Name: _____   Date: _____

Handout 8.1
Local History

Select a piece of local history from your local region/era/culture and analyze it using the following two-step process:

Step 1

Examine the piece of local history and see if you can fully answer the following questions:

- ❖ What does this piece tell you about the people who were involved it?
- ❖ What does it tell you about the time in which it occurred?
- ❖ What does it tell you about the place where it happened?
- ❖ How does it serve as an example to explain the local culture/society in this time and place?

Step 2

Using the answers and understanding from Step 1, select one of the three options to complete the analysis of the local history:

Option 1: Recreate the piece of local history in modern times in order to reflect the time, place, and culture in which you live.

Option 2: Examine a different piece of local history from the same time, place, and culture that the original piece originated from.

Format(s)

When completing Step 2 of the analysis, you are only limited by your imagination in completing the piece. Some more popular formats include: oral histories, videos and documentaries, museum displays, multimedia presentations, collection of interviews, as well as others . . . *Go forth and create!*

Annotated Bibliography

Dillard, A. (2007). *Pilgrim at Tinker Creek*. New York, NY: Harper Perennial. (Original work published in 1974)

Abstract: Annie Dillard's year spent in Virginia's Blue Ridge Valley is a boon to each and every reader who happens to stumble upon this work. Students will take away from it a definite sense of place and being. Along with these, they will understand how history can be tied to a certain geographic location.

Heat-Moon, W. L. (1999). *PrairyErth: A deep map*. New York, NY: Mariner.

Abstract: In this book, William Least Heat-Moon locates the exact geographic center of the United States and resides there for an extended amount of time. While he is there, he researches the history of the location and composes a "deep map" of it. This is one of the best examples of a professional product that matches the unit's objective.

Lopez, B. (2001). *Arctic dreams*. New York, NY: Vintage.

Abstract: Barry Lopez's beautiful and deep study of the Canadian Artic is not only a good example of this particular classroom activity, but of good writing as well. Using this text with the instructional approach is an effective means of bridging the content with science and English classes.

Chapter 9

Autobiographies, Biographies, and Memoirs: Life Writing

Introduction

The advent of the term "life writing" has coincided with its resurgence in popularity. Peruse the bestsellers list of the major newspapers and topping most all of the nonfiction lists is some piece of life writing literature. This surge in interest, across all media, is a boon for teachers.

With the rise in popular interest in what has come to be termed "life writing," academic research has expanded to incorporate this genre. A list of websites to journals and universities that support this genre is offered in Figure 9.1 for further inquiry. Opening up this genre to serious academic study has revealed that it has a symbiotic relationship with the historical era and circumstances surrounding the work(s).

Incorporating this holistic approach to studying life writing pieces gives a depth of insight to not only the author, but the era in which he or she lived and the events influenced by and influencing him or her. As such, utilizing pieces of life writing give the student a portal into not only the individual(s) who produced the item(s), but also a greater insight into the milieu that surrounds the piece(s).

Three particular subgenres of life writing are the focus of this chapter. These are autobiographies, biographies, and memoirs. The greatest challenge to this exploration is the widening breadth of media that these pieces can be presented in. Although the traditional print medium is still alive and well, the newer media of film, blogs, vlogs, and podcasts are also relevant and popular in the genre.

➢ https://www.wolfson.ox.ac.uk/clusters/life-writing/about

➢ http://ejlw.eu

➢ http://biographersinternational.org/

➢ http://www.lifewriting.com/

FIGURE 9.1. Online resources for "life writing."

Life Writing in the Classroom

More than anything, using life writing puts a human face on the event or concept being studied, and lends a particular and even at times peculiar voice. This does more to build a bridge that allows authentic learning to occur for students on a personal level. When students connect to the learning through an individual's life story, a deeper comprehension emerges. The student forms a bond with the learning because the individual's life story parallels or shares certain aspects with those of the students. In a sense, an informal community is formed utilizing this approach. When this connection is made at this particular level, then the student can begin to understand how he or she is contributing to the historical narrative.

One of the pitfalls to avoid is the "Great Man" theory of teaching social studies. This theory relies on focusing primarily on a few individuals—predominately powerful, elite White men—who have traditionally dominated social studies and history. With the broadening scope of social studies within the past three to four decades, this theory has come under close scrutiny. Instead of relying on the Great Man theory, perhaps it is time to think instead of the "Great Person" theory. Couple this with a broadening understanding of exactly what the term "great" means within the context of the social studies classroom and truly the world is wide open for examination.

How do we recognize greatness in an individual in human history? Although this is something of a bedeviling question that can lead academics into polemics, we do not have the luxury of time to decide upon a definition. Perhaps the best means of deciding the most concise measure of greatness for this particular approach is somewhat simple and straightforward. If we look to see what individuals most impacted—for better or for worse—their society, culture, and/or civilization during and after their lifetimes, this may help to determine greatness.

Classroom Activities

With this understanding arrived at, we can proceed with the activity. One famous pearl of wisdom is applicable to this study: "Don't judge someone until you have walked a mile in his or her shoes." As part of teaching social studies, this is what we struggle with daily in the classroom. Too often our students are more than proficient in judging and critiquing individuals and societies from a modern point of view. However, trying to get our students to figuratively climb into the skin of a certain individual being studied and see his or her world through his or her eyes is a Herculean task. One of the sure vehicles to arrive at this vantage point is utilizing autobiographies, memoirs, letters, and journals from these great individuals as the primary texts.

Let's take two of the suggested texts I recommend in the annotated bibliography at the end of this chapter: *I Know Why the Caged Bird Sings* by Maya Angelou and *'Tis* by Frank McCourt. Both of these best-selling works are fairly well known among the majority of students. If nothing else, students are usually at least familiar with one of the titles and authors, if not both. Both books are frank and honest descriptions of the authors' lives. As such, there are some passages that the classroom teacher will need to get clearance for from their campus administrators and department head before assigning the book. It is also recommended that a letter home to the parents precede the assignment.

Reading these texts can be done parallel to teaching the post-World War II Civil Rights era. McCourt and Angelou offer two unique and different perspectives on the same era. Focusing on different regions of the U.S. and giving different accounts, these books challenge students to see this turbulent time in American history in a new way.

Students will have the female, African-American perspective offered to them through Angelou's work, and that of the Irish immigrant, male point of view with McCourt's prose in *'Tis*. These two books offer enough material for a year's worth of discussion and writing alone. Granted, these are not the only two books that can be utilized with this particular instructional activity. Working with the campus librarian, ELA colleagues, and the department head, and even pulling titles from your own reading experiences, you will be able to match up autobiographies and memoirs with the materials in the curriculum easily.

Student Products

Now that the reading portion is completed with this particular activity, it is time for the students to create and construct a professional-level product of their own. As with some of the other instructional approaches examined in this text, this one has two options. The first of the two options is perhaps the more familiar and traditional in nature. This is the extended essay or research paper. Students can write on a prompt or topic assigned by the teacher addressing the books, historical era, and any other topics the teacher may wish to assign. The length and other requirements for this option will need to be set by the teacher beforehand.

The second option, as with the other products explored in this book, is somewhat more creative and unconventional. The students will conduct oral histories and write a short biography of someone in the school's community, or the surrounding community, playing close attention to how he or she played a role in a particular historical event. If the classroom teacher wishes to utilize this, there are a few things he or she must consider before blindly rushing into it. First and foremost, the teacher must have a firm awareness of his or her students. The teacher needs to know where his or her students are academically regarding knowledge and skills. This will help the classroom teacher better guide their students through this project. Also, the teacher needs to have a good working knowledge of the school's community for this particular project. This includes individuals both within the school's community, as in on campus, as those outside of the campus. Next, the teacher needs to plan to teach the students some basic interviewing skills.

This approach blends well with Chapter 8 because of its focus on local history. In fact, these two approaches mesh well together, borrowing in methods and products. As such, the classroom teacher could easily use one approach, such as local history, in a stair-step approach for students.

Once these few prerequisites have been met, then it is time to launch the second option. Students can interview a veteran of one of the recent wars, a survivor of a natural disaster, or someone who has weathered the hardships of the current economic downturn. These are just a few suggestions. Local museums and historical commissions are a boon of information and assistance in setting up these interviews.

After the students have collected and checked their information, they must present it. This final portion is where their creativity and ingenuity come into play. Students may present their interview material in the form of a dramatic monologue, a documentary, or a news story. It is up to their imagination and innovation. The one hard and fast rule is that they cannot manufacture or manipulate the information to fit their needs. So long as they maintain the integrity of the interview, the sky is the limit. Handout 9.1 offers some guiding questions and suggestions for student products.

Subjective:
- ➤ Style: How appealing is the piece to read? What is the pacing?
- ➤ Form: How or in what medium did the students choose to present the product?
- ➤ Language: How rich is the language used in the product?

Objective
- ➤ Research: Did the student manage to use a variety of sources outside of the norm?
- ➤ Format: How well does the product flow for the reader or audience?
- ➤ Grammar and mechanics: How free of grammatical, syntactical, and mechanical errors is the product?

FIGURE 9.2. Subjective and objective assessment categories.

Assessment

As far as assessing products, it is highly recommended that the classroom teacher adapt the general rubric provided in the appendix in order to accurately and equitably measure the students' achievement. The rubric should contain a fairly even amount of objective and subjective categories, which are presented in Figure 9.2, so that the students have an equitable chance at doing well with their products and presentations.

Handout 9.1
Writing Lives

Select a piece of life writing from a particular region/era/culture and analyze using the following two-step process:

Step 1

Examine the piece of life writing and see if you can fully answer the following questions:

❖ What does this piece tell you about the person who created it?
❖ What does it tell you about the time in which it was created?
❖ What does it tell you about the place where it was created?
❖ How does it serve as an example to explain this particular culture/society in this time and place?

Step 2

Using the answers and understanding from Step 1, select one of the three options to complete the analysis of the life writing:

Option 1: Recreate the piece of life writing in modern times in order to reflect the time, place, and culture in which you live.

Option 2: Create an original piece of life writing from the same time, place, and culture that the original piece originated from.

Option 3: Create an original piece of life writing from your own point of view/perspective.

Format(s)

When completing Step 2 of the analysis, you are only limited by your imagination in completing the piece. Some more popular formats include a dramatic monologue, a documentary, or a news story . . . ***Go forth and create!***

Annotated Bibliography

Angelou, M. (2009). *I know why the caged bird sings*. New York, NY: Ballantine. (Original work published in 1969)

Abstract: This gripping and powerful memoir by Maya Angelou meshes well with the instructional objectives of this unit. Although the content may be somewhat tough in places, the book is worth the time and effort.

McCourt, F. (1999). *'Tis: A memoir*. New York, NY: Simon & Schuster.

Abstract: The second installment of Frank McCourt's memoir trilogy not only offers up a powerful personal story, but also an excellent example of life writing. If used as a tool to teach both content and construction, it can produce some amazing results from students.

Strachey, L. (2009). *Eminent Victorians*. Oxford, England: Oxford World's Classics. (Original work published in 1918)

Abstract: This often-overlooked volume of compiled biographies by Lytton Strachey is a powerful teaching tool in the social studies classroom. Although the author's sources and analyses have been grounds for his dismissal as a serious biographer, his style and approach is priceless. Used in this unit, it is an effective vehicle for teaching life writing.

Wiesel, E. (2006). *Night*. New York, NY: Hill and Wang. (Original work published in 1955)

Abstract: This powerful autobiographical account by Elie Wiesel describes Wiesel's time in the concentration camps at Auschwitz and Buchenwald at the height of the Holocaust.

Chapter 10

Riverine History

Introduction

There is something primitive and visceral about water and the relationship between it and humanity. For the first 9 months of our lives we spend the entirety of our days in an aquatic world as our body forms and grows. Even our physical form transmogrifies through a variety of shapes to include ones that are aquatic and reptilian in nature. Water is ingrained in our DNA. In fact, we are primarily composed of liquids.

As such, history shows that early and contemporary civilizations are drawn to sources of water, and even divert water to them in order to meet their aquatic needs. Similarly, water has played a special role in numerous cultures throughout the course of human history. In particular, the role of rivers cannot be dismissed or overlooked when studying any facet of social studies seriously. This particular approach toward classroom instruction will focus on the primacy of rivers in human history, culture, and consciousness through current times. It will not only investigate quantifiable interactions between these natural highways of commerce and communication, but also address their symbolic and religious impressions upon the individual and human psyche.

There is something mysteriously alluring about a river. It is moving and fresh. Unlike its smaller cousins—the creek or lake—it is not contained or still. On the other hand, the river is miniscule compared to its ancestors, the ocean and the sea. These are where it flows to, releasing its body and offering up its soul. It is through these rivers that those who live in the middle of the continents can still be connected to the mysteries of the seas. As such, studying rivers can lead to a more metaphorical understanding of social studies. Larger than streams and creeks, but smaller than seas and oceans, rivers provide a certain safety.

Before explaining this particular approach in detail, one question or objection must be addressed in full. This classroom exploration can be successfully implemented with any level of students in any location regardless of how geographically near or far the classroom and campus are located from an actual river. In doing so, specific location in the present sense will not be a limiting factor in implementing and understanding this point of view.

Looking at the settlement patterns of ancient civilizations, it is readily apparent that rivers were necessary and vital to the health and well-being of societies. Even today, rivers play an important role in the daily lives of nations, cities, and individuals around the world. Examining the intricate roles that these bodies of water play can guide the students into a deeper and more complex perspective of not only civilization but human nature.

The River of Time in the Classroom

One of the more direct and gentler ways of introducing this particular topic to students in the social studies classroom is to begin with settlement patterns. Examining the ways in which humans established semipermanent and permanent dwellings around and near rivers is crucial in forming a foundational understanding of the relationship between humanity and rivers. This primary point of view, which underscores economic supply and demand, will help guide the students to understand the vitality of the river in the daily lives of humans.

Given the religious history of humanity, as the classroom teacher guides the students through the economic, agricultural, and historical exploration of this unique relationship between humans and rivers, it is difficult not to address its influence on society's religious understanding of the world and humanity's place in it and proper interaction with nature. The early naturist and animist religions are full of water deities. There are few cultures that do not have some god or goddess associated with water in some form or fashion.

However, those societies located close to a river system had more intricate belief and worship systems. Many scholars relate this to their reliance on agriculture, which was dependent on sustenance from the river. This is due in some part to regular, seasonal flooding that not only watered the agricultural fields but also deposited nutrient-rich soil onto the fields as well. This was a boon to the farming community and helped to ensure health and prosperity to the community. For these societies, the floods were interpreted as gifts from the deities who were pleased with the actions of the community.

There are two very familiar exemplars that can be readily utilized to guide students to this desired understanding: the ancient Egyptian civilization that thrived on the banks of the Nile River and the myriad cultures that have clung to and evolved along the banks of our own Mississippi River. Both of these examples are embedded within the popular subconscious of most students in some form or another thanks in most part to popular media. The example of the Mississippi River is part of the American mythology and folklore preserved in paintings, poems, minstrel songs, and the immortal literature of Mark Twain.

Allowing the river to tell a story and reveal its history helps develop the depth, complexity, and rigor of the narrative. Observed over time, rivers express their personalities and some of their long-held secrets to those who are attentive and patient. Many states in the Southwest, for example, have rivers that experience irregular periods of flood and slow flow. As such, the water clarity and turbidity varies widely with the seasons and the weather. This results in the river taking on and expressing a unique personality that accentuates the geography. The speed, clarity, depth, and the direction of the river are all direct parallels to better understanding depth, complexity, and rigor within the instructional context. For example, the song "Ol' Man River," made popular by Paul Robeson in the 1936 film version of the musical *Show Boat*, tells the history of the Mississippi in all of its glory and misery. Through it all, this mighty and sometimes violent river has continued to roll southward toward the Gulf of Mexico, carrying with it not only the runoff from its tributaries and sediment from the land, but the secrets from the inhabitants as well.

In fact, the Mississippi River is perhaps the best and easiest vehicle for guiding students to attaining this particular understanding and holistic perspective. Given the long-standing history and significance that the river has held throughout numerous cultures, it is a potent example of the riverine perspective that this particular classroom instructional approach is aiming toward. Achieving it not only takes time on the parts of both the students and the classroom teacher, but also must be carefully layered. Similar to the accretion action that forms sedimentary rocks, this understanding is added to layer upon layer of knowledge with a precision that is marked by time and experience like the river itself.

Similarly, the Nile River in Egypt beckons to the imagination and inquisitiveness of the classroom. This is the river that living gods traveled upon according to Egyptian mythology. It is the river that many other civilizations, such as the Greeks, Romans, and Persians, wrote about and studied. The Nile is one of the most recognized rivers in the world. Its exoticness to some is the same comfort of familiarity to others. In some grades, the Nile may be the only river available to use that both the students and the teacher are familiar with.

One of the primary concepts that the secondary social studies classroom teacher has to instill within the students is a symbolic understanding of the river as a storyline or a continuing narrative coursing through the history of a

> http://www.esri.com/what-is-gis

> http://www.noaa.gov

> http://webgis.wr.usgs.gov/globalgis

FIGURE 10.1. Resources for exploring GIS.

particular culture. This opens the door to an interdisciplinary approach that can incorporate elements from the ELA classroom.

Guiding students to a spatial understanding of the river is also important. Utilizing maps aids a great deal in arriving at this understanding. When students are able to recognize that societies established their encampments and later their cities in such proximity to rivers, the significance of rivers to humans becomes more apparent. However, what continues to mystify scholars, amateurs, and professionals alike are the deeper influences rivers have on the individual and collective psyches of these societies. The imprint rivers leave on the arts, language, music, government, literature, and other seemingly nebulous practices of societies often survives them, providing something of a living artifact for students to investigate. This is the primary focus of this instructional approach.

Classroom Activity

For the activity associated with this genre, the students will create a deep history or life story of a chosen or assigned river. This can take many different forms. For instance, students can create an annotated map, a mini-documentary, or traditional written piece. All kinds of maps are needed to pull off this part of the unit. Students need to see, touch, interpret, and analyze political, geographical, historical, and economic maps. A working knowledge of Geographic Information Systems (GIS) is crucial on the part of the teacher. Layering the data both visually and conceptually with the students helps lead the way for more complex mapping. Figure 10.1 lists some resources teachers can use to learn more about GIS.

This is an opportune time to introduce, teach, and assess geographic literacy to the students. Nationally, this is an area that is perennially weak on standardized tests among secondary students in the United States. The students will work, practice, and think like a geographer in their study of an assigned river. Their perspectives and understandings will begin to shift and broaden. This geographic knowledge is essential to move on to the other layers of comprehension.

Once students have a working knowledge of the geography of the river and its surrounding lands, it is time to take the next step, which involves using science as the primary tool of investigation. Investigating the geology, meteorology,

> http://www.rivernetwork.org

> http://www.americanrivers.org

FIGURE 10.2. Recommended online resources.

hydrology, climatology, and other environmental factors follows hand-in-hand with the foundation built by the geographic examination.

The scientific examination is one that should parallel the geographic knowledge gained in the first portion of this classroom exercise. Adding this component also affords the students the rare opportunity to experience the interdisciplinary nature of learning and education. This may take some prior planning and coordination on the parts of both the science and the social studies teachers. Complementing geographic understanding with some scientific knowledge begins to further round out the students' understanding of the riverine consciousness that the classroom teacher is guiding them toward.

For many of the students, the first two layers of understanding in this classroom exploration may be some of the easiest. The geographic and scientific perspectives are analytically based and concrete in nature. Students, especially in the middle school grades, seem to be more comfortable operating in this realm. By beginning with this frame of reference, the classroom teacher is able to start off this exploration in familiar territory.

Once these foundations have been established, the teacher will guide the students through the realm of literature. This covers a lot of territory, from oral traditions to written records. However, given the immediacy of the digital age, locating sources online is not a difficult task; Figure 10.2 offers a couple of websites that can help guide teachers.

Armed with the geographic and scientific knowledge understanding of their riverine region, the students can begin to make connections with the literature produced by individuals influenced by the flowing body of water. Again, Mark Twain's works are a resounding example of this influence and the power it had over the literature he produced throughout his lifetime.

Examining the ways in which individuals and their societies encounter and interact with the river they live beside, use to gain nourishment, utilize for commerce, and even award a central role in their religion is a formidable task for learners at any level. Literary pieces are some of the best and most accessible vehicles for studying these nebulous connections. What the classroom teacher must guide the students to making is the connection between the everyday life of the people of the river and their mental and spiritual lives as recorded in their literature. Sometimes the connections, such as with Twain, can be recognized easily, and at other times it will broaden the students' limits of comprehension and analysis.

At this point, the teacher is free to challenge students by moving the study from literature to visual arts. For this particular phase of the exploratory learning, it is recommended that the classroom teacher integrate pieces of visual art such as paintings, sculptures, drawings, and folk art pieces such as quilts and pottery. Regarding the performing arts, the teacher will want to focus more on musical pieces without lyrics and dances. With all of these, the guiding questions that drive the investigation and analysis for the students are: "How is this particular piece connected to the river?" "What and where are the influence(s) of the river apparent?" "How do those influences shape the piece?" These questions should be familiar to the students from previous phases of the instructional approach.

Student Products

A fitting and exciting summative assessment is having the students generate an original deep map of an assigned river and its immediate surrounding area. This is a project that an academic or professional geographer may be called upon to accomplish.

It is recommended that the students work in groups assigned by the teacher. Ideally, each class should be assigned a different river system than each other, and none should be assigned the river system studied in class. This project should take about five class periods to research and assemble, with the final class period a presentation day. The different groups should physically and academically layer their research and presentations on the single map. When complete, the map needs to be of museum quality with technology and interactive features included. Some interactive features could include interactive maps, videos, or computer-modeled simulations. Handout 10.1 offers some guiding questions and suggestions for student products.

Assessment

As with all the other chapters in this book, you may adapt the general rubric in the appendix to assess the student products. The following are some items that you may want include on the rubric for the products associated with this chapter:

❖ the link between geography and geology,
❖ the influence of the river on the region, and
❖ the human-environment interaction with the river.

Handout 10.1
River of Time

Select a piece of riverine history from a particular region/era/culture and analyze it using the following two-step process:

Step 1

Examine the piece of riverine history and see if you can fully answer the following questions:

- ❖ What does this piece tell you about the people who created it?
- ❖ What does it tell you about the time in which it was created?
- ❖ What does it tell you about the place where it was created?
- ❖ How does it serve as an example to explain this particular culture/society in this time and place?

Step 2

Using the answers and understanding from Step 1, select one of the three options to complete the analysis of the riverine history:

Option 1: Recreate the piece of riverine history in modern times in order to reflect the time, place, and culture in which you live.

Option 2: Examine a different piece of riverine history from the same time, place, and culture that the original piece originated from.

Option 3: Create an original piece of riverine history from a completely new and unique civilization that you have created.

Format(s)

When completing Step 2 of the analysis, you are only limited by your imagination in completing the piece. Some more popular formats include an annotated map, an original deep map, a mini-documentary, or a traditional research paper, as well as others . . . ***Go forth and create!***

Annotated Bibliography

Bowden, K. (2007). *The Tecate journals: Seventy days on the Rio Grande*. Seattle, WA: Mountaineers.

Abstract: Don't let this book's title fool you. It is actually an insightful study of the cultural, economic, and geopolitical clash surrounding the Rio Grande on the Texas/Mexico border. With gritty, personal perspective, journalist Keith Bowden leaves the reader with more questions at the end than there may have been at the start.

Heat-Moon, W. L. (2001). *River-horse: The logbook of a boat across America*. New York, NY: Penguin.

Abstract: This volume chronicling William Least Heat-Moon's continuing journey through North America is completely river-based for approximately 70 miles of portage. This transcontinental quest exemplifies the focus of this particular instructional unit.

Horgan, P. (1991). *Great River: The Rio Grande in North American history*. Middletown, CT: Wesleyan University Press.

Abstract: This two-volume set chronicling the history of the Rio Grande is priceless. Paul Horgan's deft combination of history, science, and folklore is only surpassed by his poetic style. This is a must-have for this unit, or for any secondary social studies library.

Chapter 11

Mapping History

Introduction

If there is anything that has been synonymous with social studies education throughout the ages, it is maps. Drawing them, coloring them, and memorizing them have been common practice in social studies classrooms regardless of grade level. However, despite how many maps are drawn, colored, and studied, geographic illiteracy continues to plague the United States when compared to other developed nations on standardized tests.

This concern ranks right behind science and math literacy on the list of education reforms in contemporary America. Even with a greater focus on technology and an increase in the focus on teaching geography in secondary grades, our students continue to lag behind not only in achievement but also in interest. With globalization well upon us, geographic literacy is a valuable and vital skill. So how do we better teach these skills in the secondary social studies classroom? Perhaps the more important question is how we can better engage the students to inspire and ignite a desire to become geographically literate.

Maps have been a staple of social studies education since its inception. As such, they have become somewhat overlooked. Due to their ubiquity, most social studies educators recognize them as merely a piece to a puzzle rather than a whole picture. It needs to be understood that maps are primary sources. Being able to look at a map and see past the surface information that it offers, and to appreciate it as a symbol of its time and creators is a necessary skill for an educated individual in the broadest sense.

Mapping It Out in the Classroom

One of the more exciting aspects of teaching the first half of United States history is the Lewis and Clark expedition across the newly purchased Louisiana Territory. Although the journals of the expedition's two leaders make for insightful and exciting reading, the maps made before and after the expedition tell just as exciting and penetrating a narrative.

As with any new instructional activity, the teacher should ease into reading these maps with a certain rhythm and timing that would allow the students participating to learn the concepts and skills necessary while becoming comfortable with this particular practice. This is important so that the change and challenge of reading maps can be adapted to and alleviated over time.

This genre can be complete in a 1–3-week span of time. Figure 11.1 is a sample timeline for implementing this particular instructional approach.

Classroom Activity

For this particular activity, the students will analyze a historical map in context, creating a presentation to share with the class. When looking at the Lewis and Clark Expedition with the Corps of Discovery, it is essential to study maps made by both France and Spain of the Louisiana Territory prior to the purchase in 1803. The teacher can even locate and utilize maps created by Samuel de Champlain in the 1700s. Because the territory changed hands numerous times between the French and the Spanish before the United States purchased it, the students should have a solid foundation and background from which to begin their investigation into the decoding of the maps generated by the Lewis and Clark expedition. The region originally known as the Louisiana Purchase provides ample history for the students and teacher to work with in the classroom activity.

What will jump out at most students first is the Mississippi River on all of these maps. The French, Spanish, and Americans were not only aware of this mighty natural feature, but aware of the possible economic uses and gains it had to offer whomever had control of the territory. The students should notice that more than any other natural feature of what was considered the Louisiana Territory, the Mississippi River is the most prominently featured on maps for centuries. The agricultural and subsequent economic importance of this major river system was recognized even before the arrival of Europeans in the Americas.

Another aspect of these maps to draw the students' attention to is the lack of particular natural geographic features. Once the focus moves west of the Mississippi River, the maps of this period become more and more lacking in detail until the maps reach the Pacific Ocean. Of course, the natural question

Each item below represents 2 days of class time.

➤ Introduce the topic and teach the textbook material.

➤ Discuss the different ways of making a map, and explore how to read a map from a different time period.

➤ Model the student activity in a whole-class setting.

➤ Students research and plan their product.

➤ Students complete rough and final drafts.

➤ Students present products.

FIGURE 11.1. Sample timeline.

is why these maps lacked these details. Spain, and later Mexico, explored and settled and governed this wide area. Although primarily Native American tribes (many of which were hostile toward European and American settlers) inhabited a great deal of this territory, it was not necessarily unknown territory.

Examining the maps generated by the Corps of Discovery while exploring the Louisiana Territory not only is a great way to show the unfolding of knowledge of seemingly unknown territory, but also a way to understand how "Americans" came to understand this new part of their young country. The older maps from the French and Spanish settlers have a definite European perspective and stamp of Old World geography on them. These rough drawings, which would later evolve into formal maps of the territory, are the basis for the New World cartography. If paired with written excerpts from journals and letters from the same time during the expedition, the students will have the materials to figuratively see the unspoiled land with their own eyes.

As the Corps made its way back to St. Louis on its return trip, maps were redrawn, corrected, and added to, and new were ones created. These should be compared side by side with ones made on the outward-bound journey by the brave adventurers. Again, pairing with excerpts from journals, letters, diaries, and official reports only adds depth to the students' understanding and experience. These maps would be something of an amalgamation of their writings, drawings, and surveys over the 2 years of their expedition throughout the Territory. These maps created after the Corps' return will bear the indelible mark of a new "America-ness" and a Western consciousness that would soon engulf the nation as it begun to set its sight on this virgin territory and its resources.

When the students reach this point in the instructional activity, the teacher should engage a whole-class discussion. At this point, it is time to examine all of the maps regarding this particular region. This includes the maps created prior to the Louisiana Purchase, those generated by the Corps of Discovery during its 2-year journey, and those created from the information afterward. Comparing and contrasting these maps from these three different yet closely related time periods will challenge the students to see the growth of knowledge and the birth of the West.

Student Products

After introducing this instructional activity and perspective to the students in a whole-class setting, it is recommended that the teacher divide the students into collaborative groups for products.

With this chapter, student products can include:

- ❖ a multilayered, interactive map of an assigned or chosen region,
- ❖ a dramatic monologue of the Lewis and Clarke expedition, or
- ❖ a mini-documentary that documents students as they explore an unfamiliar part of their campus or neighborhood.

Handout 11.1 offers some guiding questions for the student product.

Assessment

It is highly recommended that the classroom teacher share the rubric with the students at the onset of the unit of study so the students understand the teacher's expectations early on. The majority of misunderstandings can be cleared up at the start and less opportunity for miscommunications are likely.

Some areas that could be included in the general rubric for the products associated with this chapter are:

- ❖ Layered research: How deep did the students delve in researching their piece?
- ❖ Voice: How well do the students' personalities come through in the product?
- ❖ Creativity: How innovative and original is the product?

Name: _____   Date: _____

Handout 11.1
Mapping It Out

Select a piece of cartography (map) from a particular region/era/culture and analyze it using the following two-step process:

Step 1

Examine the map and see if you can fully answer the following questions:

❖ What does this map tell you about the people who created it?
❖ What does it tell you about the time in which it was created?
❖ What does it tell you about the place where it was created?
❖ How does it serve as an example to explain this particular culture/society in this time and place?

Step 2

Using the answers and understanding from Step 1, select one of the three options to complete the analysis of the map:

Option 1: Recreate this map in modern times in order to reflect the time, place, and culture in which you live.

Option 2: Examine a different map from the same time, place, and culture that the original piece originated from.

Option 3: Create an original map from a completely new and unique civilization that you created.

Format(s)

When completing Step 2 of the analysis, you are only limited by your imagination in completing the piece. Some more popular formats include interactive maps, videos, dramatic monologues, and others . . . ***Go forth and create!***

Annotated Bibliography

McPhee, J. (2000). *Annals of the former world.* New York, NY: Farrar, Straus and Giroux.

Abstract: This mountainous-sized geologic journey through the physical geography of the United States by John McPhee is a surprisingly enticing read. Using excerpts with students to build geographic literacy as well as visual and spatial thinking skills is an engaging activity.

Sobel, D. (2007). *Longitude: The true story of a lone genius who solved the greatest scientific problem of his time.* New York, NY: Walker & Company.

Abstract: With a journalist's eye for details and a novelist's ear for a story, Dava Sobel examines the race to determine and demark longitude on the globe. This tightly written text supports the instructional objectives of this unit.

Winchester, S. (2009). *The map that changed the world: William Smith and the birth of modern geology.* New York, NY: Harper Perennial.

Abstract: This erudite and fast-paced tale of the upending of western science is a thrilling ride through the history of science. Simon Winchester's attention to detail grabs the reader, but does not bog down the narrative. This story examines the relationship between geology and geography.

Chapter 12

Architectural History

Introduction

Architecture is an interesting and little-used vehicle for instruction in the secondary-level classroom. This is especially true in the social studies classroom. Architecture is often misunderstood as being too complex and convoluted, but if taken at its essentials, architecture is a powerful bridge in engaging students.

Architecture is tangible. It surrounds and creates the learning space. For social studies purposes, architecture is the planning, designing, and construction of structures. Keeping this definition in mind will make the incorporation of architecture a more approachable act in learning and teaching social studies.

When used this way, architecture must be understood first and foremost as an artifact. Architecture is the physical representation of human-environment interaction. As such, incorporating architecture regularly into the social studies classroom directly addresses this theme. It also opens up students to understanding how people interact and are influenced by their environment. Not only that, but there is no language barrier to contend with in studying architecture.

Building a Better History in the Classroom

This understanding leads the teacher to the inevitable questions of what this particular instructional approach would look like, how students would display mastery, and in what manner it would be assessed equitably. As explained previously, the primary activity of this instructional approach is interpreting and deciphering architecture throughout human history. The assigned curriculum will help structure the particular time, place, and peoples to be studied.

Although this instructional approach can be easily applied throughout the span of most human history, it does have its limitations. Naturally, those societies and cultures that did not construct any permanent building cannot easily be studied. However, that does not mean that they are to be completely ignored. Civilizations such as the Bedouins, nomadic traders who make their home in the forbidding Sahara Desert, can be better understood utilizing this particular classroom activity.

Continuing with this example, combining this instructional approach and focusing on architecture, the classroom teacher can guide the students through a study of the Bedouins. Mixing an investigation into the architecture of a certain place and time with a study of the religions in the same context can provide an even greater insight with a depth of understanding. The history of Islam and its prophet Mohammed and the history of the Bedouins combine to exemplify the tents and camels of the Sahara as not only signs of the Bedouin culture, but more importantly as symbols and signifiers of the religion.

Guiding students to understand architecture in this manner requires that the teacher approach social studies with a dual perspective. On one hand, the teacher must maintain a clear and objective focus of the facts and realities of history with its individuals and events. In a parallel manner, he or she must also interweave the symbolic nature of artistic expression that is at the heart of the form and function of architecture. A building is not just a building. It is an expression of the creator and constructor and a representation of its time. It is up to the classroom teacher to guide the students in gaining this perspective. The teacher needs to incorporate the ideas, opinions, movements, and religions that influenced the time and people being studied. Like art, music, and literature, these influences will be apparent in the architecture. Working as anthropologists, archaeologists, and art historians, the students will be able to uncover and analyze these influences.

Classroom Activity

With the assistance of the teacher, students will analyze their school building. They will deconstruct the design elements in order to date and place the structure within its historical context. This is extremely engaging if the school campus has portions of buildings constructed during different time periods.

Once the students have successfully navigated this architectural analysis with the guidance of the teacher, it is time for them to work in groups or on their own. It is recommended that the teacher select local buildings for the students to analyze as well. Moreover, the teacher could arrange for a field trip to a locale of architectural importance. Examples of these could be local libraries, municipal buildings, and even churches.

Student Products

The first option for a student product will be a traditional essay or research paper. Teachers may find that some students actually prefer this method of presenting their findings and analyses. The students feel more confident and safe, and it's okay to initially allow the students first to select this method of presenting their product analyzing architecture. However, it is highly recommended that if the classroom teacher continues to utilize this option, or any instructional activity from this book, that over time they guide the students away from this particular product toward more complex and challenging options.

The second option for products is more creative than the first. Again, this particular choice is up to the discretion of the classroom teacher. He or she ultimately knows the students best. The teacher can assign the students to design a modern version of the construction being studied from the students' own cultures and point of view. For instance, the teacher could have the students design columns from their own point of view with unique hieroglyphs. This would require a certain amount of preplanning on the teacher's part. Regardless of the product, the primary focus is guiding students through an understanding of the influence the geography has on the physical structures. Handout 12.1 offers some more suggestions for student products.

Assessment

In assessing the students' products for this classroom approach, utilizing the generic rubric provided is a simple and effective means of objectively measuring the students' achievement. The following areas should be added to the rubric in order to address the students' products adequately:

- ❖ Research: How deep did the students delve into the building and architectural details?
- ❖ Creativity: How inventive was the students' products?
- ❖ Approach: How well did the students' products engage the audience?

Handout 12.1
Architectural History

Select a piece of architecture from a particular region/era/culture and analyze using the following two-step process:

Step 1

Examine the piece of architecture and see if you can fully answer the following questions:

❖ What does this construct tell you about the people who created it?
❖ What does it tell you about the time in which it was created?
❖ What does it tell you about the place where it was created?
❖ How does it serve as an example to explain this particular culture/society in this time and place?

Step 2

Using the answers and understanding from Step 1, select one of the three options to complete the analysis of the architecture:

Option 1: Recreate the piece of architecture in modern times in order to reflect the time, place, and culture in which you live.

Option 2: Examine a different piece of architecture from the same time, place, and culture that the original piece originated from.

Option 3: Create an original piece of architecture from a completely new and unique civilization that you have created.

Format(s)

When completing Step 2 of the analysis, you are only limited by your imagination in completing the piece. Some more popular formats include models, comic strips, videos, poster and PowerPoint presentations, and others . . . *Go forth and create!*

Annotated Bibliography

Gross, M. (2006). *740 Park: The story of the world's richest apartment building*. New York, NY: Broadway.

Abstract: This unique work by Michael Gross works as a biography of the tony apartment building located at 740 Park Avenue in New York City. The structure and focus of this book serves as a powerful example of the product the students are working to produce at the end of this unit.

Jonnes, J. (2008). *Conquering Gotham: Building Penn Station and its tunnels*. New York, NY: Penguin.

Abstract: Penn Station was considered one of the iconic New York City landmarks before being demolished in 1960. Jill Jonnes's study examines how architecture endures overtime, capturing a moment and anchoring a place for generations.

King, R. (2013). *Brunelleschi's dome: How a Renaissance genius reinvented architecture*. London, England: Bloomsbury Books.

Abstract: Ross King is a master of Renaissance architecture and art history. This book vibrates with King's signature nimble prose, examining the pivotal role architecture played in the Renaissance, as well as in the continuing narrative of human history.

Chapter 13

Religions Throughout History

Introduction

For many individuals, it may seem as though the current tension and level of anxiety between the West and the Middle East is at a point where it may possibly be too late to cultivate meaningful dialogue to promote peaceful relations. However, a close scrutiny of the overall historical narrative between not only the Middle East and the West, but also between major civilized regions, reveals that tensions and hostilities between major societies have populated human history around the world since the birth of civilization.

Whenever two differing societies have encountered one another, there has been a consistent pattern of disagreement that inevitably leads to friction between these groups of people. Examining these conflicts through the lens of history, the conclusion becomes apparent that misunderstanding and miscommunication were the roots of the majority of these conflicts. Myths and misconceptions often fueled rage and rancor on the battlefield. Exploring the advent, evolution, and role of religions in the societies that they served—and in many places, continue to serve—helps to give a unique insight into a particular people, place, and time. Religion leaves its distinctive brand upon each of the individuals and places it has inhabited. Given the deep-seated beliefs and traditions embedded within religions, it is important to make sure that an objective perspective is maintained.

Regardless of the religion being examined, the belief system will give clues to pertinent facets of its particular place in geography and history. However, before delving into any academic study of any religion, certain ground rules

> ❑ Establish a respectful framework for discussions.
>
> ❑ Create an understanding that this study is to understand and appreciate, not to criticize.
>
> ❑ Regularly remind the students that religion is being looked at as an artifact, and the goal is not to win converts.
>
> **FIGURE 13.1.** Checklist for guiding religious history discussions.

must be established within the classroom in order to safely direct the inquiry and investigations of the students and the teachers. Given the sometimes volatile nature of religious studies within the realm of public education, an established and defined framework with a protocol for exploring religion in the classroom makes implementing this instructional approach more pleasant. These protocols help ease the anxieties of campus and district administrators as well as parents. Sharing this framework well in advance of initiating the study will go further in securing and strengthening this classroom investigation than perhaps anything else the teacher could ever do. Figure 13.1 provides a checklist for teachers to help them safely guide discussions of religious history in the classroom.

Religious History in the Classroom

Once the teacher has taken those points into consideration, he or she can proceed without too many impediments. In all actuality, the Torah, the Bible, and the Quran are the main pieces of classroom materials needed to commence this academic exploration. As with any new instructional approach, the classroom teacher should be familiar with the histories and scriptures of the religions in order to guide the students through them. This means the teachers should have read through the writings at least once and perhaps some commentaries as well before teaching them. It is not expected that the classroom teacher be a theological expert in any shape or form.

As the classroom teacher guides the students through the religion, there are some crucial connections that the students need assistance in making. Ultimate among these connections is seeing the relationship between the facets of a particular religion and the geographical region in which it manifested, as well as the civilization that bore it. Religions are living relationships between humanity and its environment. As such, by investigating the origin, development, and interactions between religions, students can get a unique insight into the interactions between humans and their surroundings.

A simple example of this relationship is easily found in ancient Egypt. Given the geographic location of this wonderful civilization, its survival depended the annual flooding of the Nile River to sustain crops. As such, much of the ancient Egyptian theology was based on seasonal cycles and agriculture. This is most evident in Egyptian stories of the birth, death, and rebirth cycle. Like many other religions of its time, the ancient Egyptians had their share of violent stories in which gods and goddesses clashed over control of territory and riches. Like the humans they lorded over, the Egyptian deities could be just as capricious.

This human element added to the supernatural powers of the deities gives an effective and manageable bridge for students to traverse in order to make a connection with past cultures. Moreover, both the human and supernatural qualities of the deities combine in a unique way that unlocks the relationship the society maintained with its environment. More than anything, this is the overall key to the entire academic investigation. Exploring religions within their geographic and historical contexts allows students to examine these beliefs systems in an objective manner without attaching many emotional ties to them. It also allows the teacher to guide his or her students through the investigation and analysis without running too great of a risk of upsetting parents and administrators in the process. The next natural step in this process is having the students produce a product and assessing their work in order to measure growth and achievement.

Although many of the instructional approaches shared in this book offer the teacher a variety of professional-level opportunities to challenge and excite the critical and creative minds of his or her students, this particular one takes more of a traditional stance. Perhaps the most effective product to challenge the students with is an academic analysis. Although this may not seem like the most creative approach to having the students produce a professional or collegiate-level product, maintaining high expectations, as good classroom teachers do, for the students' written analyses does usually result in a critical and creative output. In this sense, the students explore and display their talents in a traditional academic venue. However, some nontradtional products are offered in the "Student Products" section on the next page.

Classroom Activity

In this classroom activity, students will be analyzing a particular world religion and creating a poster presentation or dramatic monologue that exemplifies the "story" of the religion they investigated. Keeping with this approach, the students will analyze the interrelationship between the culture, religion, and an assigned geographic region where these living artifacts sprang up. When assessing and measuring these analyses, it is up to the classroom teacher to authentically and genuinely assess them. Looking at the students' classwork and products individually gives the classroom teacher a better understanding and perspective of the students' achievements and progress within this specific context.

Taking an objective approach to exploring and analyzing religions of the world is an inviting and inquiry-based approach to igniting the curiosity of students. Helping them by guiding through the connections between the people, beliefs, and geography may assist in provoking insights into these seemingly foreign perspectives. Doing so can help to build understanding where once ignorance led.

Student Products

The primary goal of student products is to have students analyze and synthesize the religion(s) being studied. Students should be able to make connections between the religion(s) studied within the historical and geographic contexts. Like the previous chapter concerning architecture, religious history is an artifact. Students are challenged to see how people in a certain place and time understand their place in the universe as well as their relationship to it.

Students can display this understanding in a variety of forms. There is the traditional written report, which does satisfy the need to grade work. However, it does not necessarily challenge students. One way to combat this is to provide a nontraditional product. This can include generating graphic designs to represent the interaction between humans and their surroundings, or creating a diorama that illustrates religious diaspora through a certain region of the world. Handout 13.1 offers some guiding questions for students.

Assessment

The general rubric provided in this book's appendix can be easily adapted to fit these products. What's important to watch for is the students' objectivity in presenting their investigated religions—the presentations should be expository, and students should not use this as an opportunity to preach or convert. Students should focus on the historical and geographic context surrounding their religions.

Name: _____   Date: _____

Handout 13.1
Religious History

Select a religion from a particular region/era/culture and analyze using the following two-step process:

Step 1

Examine the religion and see if you can fully answer the following questions:

❖ What does this religion tell you about the people who created it?
❖ What does it tell you about the time in which it was created?
❖ What does it tell you about the place where it was created?
❖ How does it serve as an example to explain this particular culture/society in this time and place?

Step 2

Using the answers and understanding from Step 1, select one of the three options to complete the analysis of the religion:

Option 1: Recreate the religion in modern times in order to reflect the time, place, and culture in which you live.

Option 2: Examine a different religion from the same time, place, and culture that the original piece originated from.

Option 3: Create an original religion from a completely new and unique civilization that you have created.

Format(s)

When completing Step 2 of the analysis, you are only limited by your imagination in completing the piece. Some more popular formats include graphic novels, dioramas, comic strips, videos, dramatic monologues, and others . . . ***Go forth and create!***

Annotated Bibliography

Campbell, J. (1991). *The masks of God*. New York, NY: Penguin.

Abstract: Although Joseph Campbell continues to be something of a controversial figure in certain academic circles even many years after his passing, there is no denying the insightfulness and enlightenment of his teachings. This trilogy is a thorough examination of Eastern and Western mythologies. Time and place play crucial roles in the creation and faces of these mythologies.

Smith, H. (2009). *The world's religions*. New York, NY: HarperOne. (Original work published in 1958)

Abstract: When it comes to an even-handed, objective approach to studying the world's religious traditions, Huston Smith is your best bet. This particular text is one of the best single-volume resources to have in a secondary social studies classroom.

Chapter 14

History Through Art

Introduction

One of the most challenging aspects currently facing the classroom teacher concerns English language learners (ELLs). Students whose native language is one other than English comprise the core foundation of this population. However, socioeconomic status is slowly coming into recognition as an exacerbating factor that inhibits English language competency and comprehension. As such, a greater number of students with limited English vocabularies are coming into the classrooms with a monumental challenge facing them. Not only are these students expected to digest and incorporate the content knowledge and skills that they are exposed to in their classes, but also to master a grade-level vocabulary that they may be months or years behind on through little fault of their own. As such, incorporating art and artifacts from the various time periods studied in the social studies class will assist the teacher in overcoming this linguistic challenge and guide the students through differentiated instruction to a greater level of depth and complexity.

Picturing History in the Classroom

This instructional methodology is especially effective in challenging advanced-level or gifted students. Perhaps even more appealing is that this particular instructional approach immediately corresponds to the growing ELL population in our gifted and talented programs throughout the nation. With the majority of our students coming into the classroom with either a limited academic vocabulary or one with gaps, incorporating visual educational experiences helps to remove these roadblocks to learning. It also helps to build student confidence in a variety of aspects.

Including art and art history in the social studies classroom is a powerful measure in cultivating an environment for student success. Simple engagements with works of visual art are potent vehicles for engaging otherwise disinterested and reluctant students. Most every student likes to doodle. By incorporating paintings, illustrations, and sculptures into the context of social studies, the teacher is taking a large step in humanizing history and geography. Visual art is the expression of emotions. Emotions are universal and timeless and can be communicated across all languages. The classroom teacher does not have to be an expert in art or art history to enjoy implementing this instructional approach.

Classroom Activity

The first step in implementing this particular instructional approach is providing the students with a survey of the context in which they will encounter the pieces of visual art. Students may choose a particular time period, artistic style, or artist to analyze one piece of art or artifact; alternatively, the teacher can assign a time period or style that fits the social studies content being covered at the time. Condensed biographies, timelines, and surveys of the historical era are effective tools for introducing the art's backstory to the students. It is not necessary for the classroom teacher to know or to teach particular methods of critiquing art. The objective is to get students to interact with the piece(s) as artifacts and exemplars of a particular place and time.

After researching timelines and biographies, the students are ready to face a piece of art or artifact. In a certain sense, the student now takes on the role of an archaeologist. Armed with background information to assist in the analysis, translation, and deconstruction of the piece, the student can feel confident in successfully engaging the piece of art or artifact.

At this point in the learning exercise, the student needs to utilize some form of a thinking graphic or brainstorming technique. One of the most effective means of implementing this portion of the instructional approach is to walk through it with the students in a whole-group activity using a piece of art. As with any new instructional approach or classroom learning activity, this is a vital step in giving the students the scaffolding they need in order to be successful. This think-aloud and group practice is the best time to make mistakes and ask questions of the students. Figure 14.1 lists some suggested questions to use in guiding students through their encounters with their art pieces.

> ➤ Who was/were the artist(s)?

> ➤ What do you see in the work of art?

> ➤ How does it make you feel? What reactions did you have looking at it?

> ➤ When was the piece produced? What was happening at the time?

> ➤ What historical/geographic clues are present in the piece of art?

> ➤ Why is the piece representative of this particular individual/event/era?

> ➤ How might the time and place have influenced the artist(s)?

> ➤ What message do you think the artist was trying to communicate?

> ➤ What evidence of the artist's message—if there is one—do you see?

> ➤ How does the piece help generate a better understanding of the individual/ event/era?

FIGURE 14.1. Guiding questions for analyzing artwork.

From this point, it would be a good measure to group the students and have them choose the piece of art or artifact they will be working with. Have the students form their groups and have each one brainstorm the assigned or chosen piece. Although the students will work in collaborative groups, they will be responsible for completing an individual critique/brainstorm sheet, which they can make in whatever format suits them best on a blank sheet of paper. It is recommended that the teacher generate the guiding question for the learning exercise. However, after a few formative experiences, the teacher could open the discussion up to the class. This would be appropriate after an introductory discussion or lesson over the historical event or era.

Student Products

Ultimately, the final product of this learning experience will be something that synthesizes the students' analyses and critiques of the artwork to produce a distinctive understanding and perspective on not only the piece of art, but the historical era in which it was produced as well. Although this can serve as the culminating exercise for the lesson, this is especially recommended for beginning implementation in the classroom and can also serve as a foundational exercise that the students can build upon in subsequent class sessions.

The first option is to assign a modified form of the guiding question, making it more open-ended, to the students requiring a formal essay response. With this application, the students are challenged to put their critiques and analyses into a more formalized writing format, and they also have the opportunity to strengthen their writing skills to include grammar, mechanics, and spelling. Although this is a more traditional format for the student products, it is a necessary and affective approach to student success.

The second option is completely left up to the classroom teachers as to whether they wish to implement it or not. Unlike some of the other products, this one is not as limited by student language acquisition. In fact, this product can be used without implementing the writing portions described earlier. The students will generate an original piece of art reflecting an assigned historical period, events, individuals, ideas, or movements. This will allow students to critically and creatively engage the content knowledge they are studying and show a mastery of comprehension, analysis, and evaluation of the subject. Just as the project allows for broad latitude regarding content and media, the classroom teacher will enjoy similar freedom in assigning and assessing the product. This last student product is flexible enough to be encapsulated within a single class period or days depending upon the depth the teacher is looking for and how much time the curriculum allows for. Handout 14.1 offers some guiding questions and more product suggestions.

Assessment

When looking at the student-generated pieces, an important factor in accurately and effectively assessing these pieces is focusing on the content and analysis of the works. Due to the subjectivity of art as a whole, the form and style are difficult aspects of the product and can be somewhat problematic. In order to sidestep these unnecessary issues, it is recommended that the teacher adapt the general grading rubric and discuss it prior to the commencement of the actual artistic product. It is further recommended that the criteria of "style," "art," and "creativity" should not be included on the rubric. Instead the focus should be on the analysis, evaluation, and response expressed in the product.

Handout 14.1
Picturing History

Select a piece of art from a particular region/era/culture and analyze using the following two-step process:

Step 1

Examine the piece of art and see if you can fully answer the following questions:
- ❖ What does this piece tell you about the people who created it?
- ❖ What does it tell you about the time in which it was created?
- ❖ What does it tell you about the place where it was created?
- ❖ How does it serve as an example to explain this particular culture/society in this time and place?

Step 2

Using the answers and understanding from Step 1, select one of the three options to complete the analysis of the art:

Option 1: Recreate the piece of art in modern times in order to reflect the time, place, and culture in which you live.

Option 2: Examine a different piece of art from the same time, place, and culture that the original piece originated from.

Option 3: Create an original piece of artwork from a completely new and unique civilization that you have created.

Format(s)

When completing Step 2 of the analysis, you are only limited by your imagination in completing the piece. Some more popular formats include essays, sculptures, drawings, videos, paintings, collages, and others . . . ***Go forth and create!***

Annotated Bibliography

Pachter, M. (2006). *Portrait of a nation*. New York, NY: Merrell.

Abstract: This volume is a collection of highlights from the National Portrait Gallery of the Smithsonian Institute. Included with the reproductions is some background information, but additional research will be required. The vibrant volume strongly supports the learning outcomes in this unit.

Perry, L. (2006). *History's beauties: Women and the National Portrait Gallery, 1856–1900*. Surrey, United Kingdom: Ashgate.

Abstract: Although this is definitely one of the more expensive texts shared in this bibliography, it is worth the price for the reproductions alone. This is especially true if you can find a used copy in good condition. This volume does contain more background information as well as critical analyses.

Chapter 15

Death and Dying Throughout History

Introduction

Death comes to us all. This is an inescapable and universal fact of life. Even though this aspect of life seems so far from the thoughts of most adolescents and young adults, it does seem to capture their imaginations. The breaking up of young love, the untimely death of family members, and even the rare instances of classmates dying keep the specter of death hovering near youth and innocence. As such, discussing the understanding and treatment of death by different cultures in different places and during different times provides an interesting point of view into various societies during particular eras.

Even with all of our technological advances, death maintains its mysterious nature. It beguiles and bewitches us. It is a mystery that continues to capture the imaginations of us all with an immediacy that few other topics do. Much of the mythologies created in humanity's past are concerned with death, with what comes after it, or with cheating its seemingly inescapable hold. Religions offer succor and peace surrounding the finitude of bodily existence. For those who choose to reject these spiritual understandings of existence, science continues to push the boundaries of physical life at the cellular level in order to cheat death of its due. Yet, this final stage of life still collects its toll.

Death and Dying in the Classroom

Death is a difficult subject at any age. Bringing the topic of death into the classroom adds a challenge for any teacher, not to mention the students. It may be helpful to guide the students through a remembrance of friends and family who have passed away. This can be from something as simple as a journal entry, to the creation of a paper memorial for their deceased. This topic, however uncomfortable, needs to be addressed before going forward with this particular classroom instructional approach and activity. However, the class does not need to morph into a therapy session. The key is paying homage to the passed and moving on to the study of death and dying throughout the world and historical eras.

When implementing this particular instructional approach in the secondary social studies classroom, it is necessary for the teacher to discuss the topic. Like the previous chapter using world religions, the teacher needs to establish that death and dying will be explored objectively. Students need to understand that since death and dying are universal experiences; they provide powerful opportunities to explore the perspectives of life and the afterlife of societies at a particular place and time.

Classroom Activity

For this classroom instructional approach, students will be asked to delve into the mysterious understanding that a particular culture had about death and dying during a specific era. In a sense, the funerary rites and beliefs are to be studied as artifacts. Discussing death and the journey of dying, first as a whole group and then in small or individual groups, should serve as an introduction to this activity. However, as stated earlier, it does not need to dominate the entire lesson cycle.

In order to effectively communicate and engage their audience during the presentation phase, students can be challenged by creating a memorial for the society that they are studying within the time period. For instance, a coffin for the American society during the 20th century could be a fitting symbol so long as pictures accompany it. During the presentation portion, students will explain the significance of their design.

Once the students have moved from whole-class to either small-group or individual investigations and explorations, the classroom teacher is presented with a few crucial decisions. The first of these is whether to allow students to select a society or civilization to research or to assign one. The next obvious step is to determine if the students will work in collaborative groups or individually. Again, the classroom teacher will know best as to which one of these options is the best fit for their classroom setting and student population.

Student Products

As to the actual product, there are two distinct and practical means of challenging and assessing the students' understanding of the concept and content. The first of these two options limits the students to an academic synthesis of their knowledge of the civilization with the focus on death and the rituals surrounding dying. The products would be comprised of traditional works such as papers and presentations.

However, with the changing expectations provided by state and national standards, these more traditional approaches to student products do not always generate cognitive skills that will better serve students in the postsecondary and professional arenas. Taking the academic and cognitive challenge up another notch for the students in order to better prepare them, this second option allows students to take a sampling of civilizations and generate a comparative analysis of their understanding of death and rituals surrounding dying. From this particular analysis, the students will create a new and unique perspective of these civilizations and societies. With this perspective, the students will add to the existing body of material, but not necessarily through traditional writing and publication. Students can create original artwork, dramatic pieces, poetry, music, dance, and even documentaries to share with the class and even perhaps the rest of the grade and the campus. Handout 15.1 offers some guiding questions and product suggestions for students.

Assessment

Although anything creative in nature can be difficult to grade, the focus on grading should be in two areas. It is recommended that the classroom teacher focus the grading on the students' content knowledge and communication skills present in the product. Sharing the rubrics at the beginning of the unit are the best means of clearing up and avoiding misunderstandings and communication errors before they crop up along the way.

Rubrics will be discussed in further detail at the end of the book. This will help the classroom teacher better set up the unit and prepare to implement the particular classroom approach for secondary social studies. More than anything, it must be borne in mind by the teacher and modeled at all times that this is both engaging and enjoyable even though death and dying is not necessarily the most uplifting of subjects.

Handout 15.1
Death and Dying

Select a piece of custom regarding death and dying from a particular region/era/culture and analyze using the following two-step process:

Step 1

Examine the piece and see if you can fully answer the following questions:
- ❖ What does this piece tell you about the people who created it?
- ❖ What does it tell you about the time in which it was created?
- ❖ What does it tell you about the place where it was created?
- ❖ How does it serve as an example to explain this particular culture/society in this time and place?

Step 2

Using the answers and understanding from Step 1, select one of the three options to complete the analysis of the piece:

Option 1: Recreate the piece in modern times in order to reflect the time, place, and culture in which you live.

Option 2: Examine a different piece regarding death and dying from the same time, place, and culture that the original piece originated from.

Option 3: Create an original piece regarding death and dying from a completely new and unique civilization that you have created.

Format(s)

When completing Step 2 of the analysis, you are only limited by your imagination in completing the piece. Some more popular formats include rituals, poetry, dances, videos, dramatic monologues, artwork, music, and others . . . **Go forth and create!**

Annotated Bibliography

Fulghum, R. (1996). *From beginning to end*. New York, NY: Ivy.

Abstract: America's unacknowledged philosopher laureate takes readers through rituals at the different points in our lives. This book gives a humane and sometimes humorous look at end of life issues.

Lynch, T. (2009). *The undertaking: Life studies from the dismal trade*. New York, NY: W. W. Norton.

Abstract: Thomas Lynch is an undertaker by training and by trade. This award-winning poet and essayist utilizes his unique perspective as well as his uncanny way with words to explore our society's changing relationship with death and dying. This book directly supports both the focus and objectives of this unit.

Mitford, J. (2000). *The American way of death revisited*. New York, NY: Vintage.

Abstract: This groundbreaking book pulled back the mysterious veil on the little-known profession of undertaking and funerary services. This updated version only enhances the original.

Chapter 16

Caricatures Throughout History

Introduction

Caricatures have been used since early history in satirizing events and people in history, as well as expressing opinions. The art of the caricature is actually a time-honored tradition. Caricature uses exaggeration as well as understatement to relate what is many times an opposing or dissenting opinion of the dominant point of view. Caricature allows an individual to speak or show dissent or opposition in a fairly nonthreatening way. However, just how scathing and satirical the caricature is meant to be is up to the artist creating the caricature.

Caricature is an artifact representing a particular society, during a particular era, in a particular place. With this unique understanding, caricature opens up powerful opportunities in the social studies classroom. These visual artifacts are just as insightful and endearing as the works of visual art described in an earlier chapter. One of the facets of caricature that makes it appealing to students is that it is both humorous and open to all audiences. Anyone who can doodle and is paying attention to current events is able to create caricatures.

Caricatures in the Classroom

A certain understanding and appreciation for the practice and process of caricature must be attained in the classroom before beginning any activity. The earliest identifiable individual caricaturist was Leonardo Da Vinci. This icon of the Renaissance was known to seek out individuals with physical deformities in order to sketch them. Supposedly, Da Vinci's purpose in using these individuals as his models was to capture a more authentic impression and expression of the person, both inside and out. He believed that this would be more genuine than what the subject would present during a formal portrait sitting.

Establishing a framework to effectively operate within would further assist both the students and the teacher. The caricaturist has to first decide whether his or her current work is meant to amuse and entertain the audience, or if it is a political or social commentary. This is absolutely vital in setting the tone for the entire production of the caricature. Regardless of the artist's approach or answer, the end result of a caricature is mockery. The tone or flavor of the mockery will be directly tied to the artist's intended use. If the caricature is intended for serious political/social commentary, then it will more than likely be scathing.

The caricaturist needs to focus on the subject's natural characteristics. For example, this may be large ears as with Lyndon B. Johnson, the large nose and jowls of Richard Nixon, or the gangly height of Abraham Lincoln. The second aspect a caricaturist focuses on is "acquired characteristics." These would be mannerisms and behaviors that prominent individuals have acquired and make them readily available in the piece. Examples of this would be Winston Churchill's distinctive cigars or Salvador Dali's unique moustache. The third and final focus has to do with perhaps the most human of all qualities: the vanities of the subject being mocked. An excellent example of this is the elongated cigarette holder and wire rimmed eye glasses used by Franklin D. Roosevelt, or the famous corn cob pipe, aviator's sun glasses, and officer's hat indicative of General MacArthur. All of these combined make for an effective and engaging caricature.

Naturally, the questions that arise at this point are how and when you would implement the particular instructional approach, and what a classroom activity looks like. In order to guide students to producing their own original caricatures at or near the professional level, they should have an appreciation for the art form.

With respect to the classroom, this particular instructional approach and curricular activity can be effectively implemented into most any content area and grade at the secondary level.

Classroom Activity

Students will have the opportunity to display their creative talents in a simple and straightforward way: drawing. Most of the time, classroom teachers have a dilemma in keeping students on track while either engaged in direct teaching or practice activities. This approach is one way to get students thinking both critically and creatively while ensconced in the content material. The annotated bibliography section of this chapter includes a link appropriate for the exploration portion of the activity.

With this approach, it is not recommended to just let the students loose after looking at a few samples. It is paramount for student success that they understand the nature of caricature. While looking at samples, which include editorial cartoons from newspapers and magazines, it is important that the teacher guides the students' understanding that the exaggeration of individuals' physical characteristics is a vehicle for pointing out character traits, both good and bad.

As such, when first working on caricatures, both students and teachers need to study caricatures as a means of communication. In fact, it is beneficial for students to copy practitioners in the field. Like painters and writers, students will be able to get a feel for the art and craft of caricaturing. This is also an opportune time for the social studies teacher to team up with colleagues in the English department. Studying caricature alongside fables can be powerful in guiding students to a deeper appreciation and understanding of these two art forms.

Student Product

It is not surprising that students will be generating a portfolio of caricatures during this instructional activity. However, what is important is that they are able to communicate the meanings of their caricatures in class. In order to spare embarrassment for both students and teachers, it is recommended that the teacher assign a historical era as well as a geographic place, location, and/or region for the students to work within.

The end product from this classroom activity is a portfolio of caricatures created by the students. Along with the caricatures, the students will have to provide short written explanations of their pieces. Included in these explanations are the reasons why they chose the individuals they did for the caricatures. Also, students will need to explain their choice for caricature. For example, why they selected a large nose for someone who was a famous liar is part of the written component. In all, the students should be assigned to produce approximately six pieces of caricature.

As with the majority of the classroom activities explored in this text, this one incorporates a classroom presentation of the students' products. For the sake of class time, it is recommended that the students be limited to two or three pieces from their portfolio so that attention does not wane and classroom management becomes an issue. Some time should be allotted for question and answer sessions after each presentation. Handout 16.1 offers some guiding questions and format suggestions for students.

Assessment

It is recommended that the teacher utilize the general rubric provided in the appendix. Most of the scoring categories will remain the same. However, there are two categories that need to be focused on when assessing students' portfolios: research and creativity.

Research is a fairly straightforward aspect of the products to assess. The main idea behind this category is to see how "deep" the students took their research of the individuals, events, and regions that they were either assigned or selected. Student selection should only be attempted after conducting this instructional approach a couple of times. For research, the students need to look past fast websites and easy materials. An example of this could be a biography of the person, or primary sources from the time period.

Creativity is an aspect of assessment that most teachers shy away from. It is difficult for individuals to measure the creativity of someone else. However, when it is coupled with something like research, creativity is not such a nebulous item. Building on the foundation of "deep" research, the teacher should assess how unique and original the students' approach to their subjects is. For example, did the students use something like thick glasses to characterize an individual who made rash decisions? The subject's shortsightedness and lack of forethought is communicated in this way.

Handout 16.1
Content Caricatures

Select a caricature from a particular region/era/culture and analyze using the following two-step process:

Step 1

Examine the caricature and see if you can fully answer the following questions:

❖ What does this piece tell you about the people who created it?
❖ What does it tell you about the time in which it was created?
❖ What does it tell you about the place where it was created?
❖ How does it serve as an example to explain this particular culture/society in this time and place?

Step 2

Using the answers and understanding from Step 1, select one of the three options to complete the analysis of the caricature:

Option 1: Create a portfolio of original caricatures with written explanations for each.

Format(s)

When completing Step 2 of the analysis, you are only limited by your imagination in completing the piece. Caricatures don't necessarily have to be drawn. You can make a video, audio recording, or even sculpture . . . *Go forth and create!*

Annotated Bibliography

Redman, L. (1984). *How to draw caricatures*. New York, NY: McGraw-Hill.

Abstract: This text takes a very practical approach to learning and drawing caricatures. In some aspects, Lenn Redman's text parallels the one below by Mitchell Smith. The text offers practical advice on seeing the world in caricature and drawing it. Redman offers a little more in-depth explanation of caricatures as well as practical advice than Smith's does.

Smith, M. (2007). *The art of caricaturing: Making comics*. New York, NY: BN Publishing.

Abstract: This is a valuable resource for implementing caricaturing in the social studies classroom. The text's straightforward style appeals to every level of reader. Also, some of the examples given are wonderful in teaching history.

The following websites are useful for learning about the history and practice of caricatures:

❖   http://www.courtjones.com
❖   http://neuro-caricatures.eu/leonardos-grotesque

Chapter 17

Coining the Past and Present

Introduction

Even with the ever-increasing use of debit and credit cards to pay bills and purchase goods, there is still something noteworthy and nostalgic about the use of coined money. Coins are daily witnesses to history as both art and artifact. Learning to listen to their own unique and particular language, we can tease their stories from them and perhaps a bit of wisdom along the way.

Coins, for this instructional approach and classroom activity, serve as exemplars unlocking the time, place, and people who minted and used them. With this perspective in mind, coins will serve as guides to examining the cultures and civilizations being studied. The pressings, metals, and the sizes of the coins are all markers to be read and deciphered. Working, thinking, and behaving in this particular manner challenges students to operate and function as archaeologists and numatists (i.e., coin collectors) in the classroom.

Coining the Past and Present in the Classroom

As with any new, content-based instructional approach, it is necessary that the classroom teacher have a fundamental working knowledge of the subject matter. Although it is not necessary for the teacher to be an encyclopedic expert on coins and any other form of currency, he or she must at least have a level of competency to comfortably guide the students through the classroom activity.

The annotated bibliography at the end of this chapter offers some resources for both teachers and students.

Classroom Activity

To begin with, the classroom teacher may want to take the students through a coin analysis. As such, something like the new state quarters or the bicentennial nickels of the Lewis and Clark expedition are two powerful pieces to use. Look at the coins with the students, and ask questions as to why the designers chose the symbols they did. Follow up with a query on the importance of the symbols. Then, challenge the students with the selection of the numeric value.

Implementing this unique instructional approach and classroom activity in the social studies classroom in which United States history is studied is a fairly easy fit. Within this particular spectrum of history, the presidents George Washington, Thomas Jefferson and Abraham Lincoln are incorporated on the traditional quarter, nickel, and penny. The newer minted ones with the commemorative designs can be utilized as well. Students will be examining the insignia on each coin, and writing down or discussing what they think these symbols represent in the context of U.S. history.

This activity is a particularly powerful means of cultivating an interdisciplinary or cross-curricular atmosphere within the learning environment itself. In particular, utilizing coins from around the world and throughout history incorporates the core content areas of science as well as the essential elective courses of art and foreign languages.

The following is a list of suggested guiding questions that can be used as students examine and research their coins:

❖ Why do you think these images are important to this society?
❖ What meaning do this shape, value, and/or design of this particular coin hold for this society?
❖ Where would this society have obtained this metal, and why do you think they used it for coining/minting money?
❖ What does this artifact tell us about the society that used it?
❖ What questions does this artifact leave unanswered, and what questions does it generate?

Student Products

The products for this activity are fairly straightforward. The students will be designing their own coined currency for a particular place, location, and/or region, during a particular historical period, created by a specific group of people.

These newly created coins do not need to be made of metal. In fact, the students can select whatever material they think is appropriate for the currency. They must, however, include symbols and writing that are significant and symbolic of their assigned people, place, and time. Challenge the students to generate models of their currency.

During the final class day of this classroom activity, the students will present their products. Included in the presentation will be either drawings or models of the coined currency and an explanation of the markings on them. The students should make clear connections with the designs as well as the value of their coined currency during the presentation. These should reflect the people, places, and times that they were assigned by the teacher. Handout 17.1 offers guiding questions and product options for students.

Assessment

When the time arrives to measure the students' products, it is highly recommended that the classroom teacher employ the general rubric provided in the book's appendix. Strong emphasis should be placed on the link between the students' coins and their assigned region/culture/era. Some students might see the product as an excuse to draw, but be sure students have actual research to support their coin design.

Handout 17.1
Coining History

Select a coin(s) or money from a particular region/era/culture and analyze using the following two step process:

Step 1

Examine the piece of coin(s)/money and see if you can fully answer the following questions:

❖ What does this piece tells you about the people who created it?
❖ What does it tell you about the time in which it was created?
❖ What does it tell you about the place where it was created?
❖ How does it serve as an example to explain this particular culture/society in this time and place?

Step 2

Using the answers and understanding from Step 1, select one of the three options to complete the analysis of the coin(s)/money:

Option 1: Recreate the piece of coin(s)/money in modern times in order to reflect the time, place, and culture in which you live, so that it is able to answer the same questions from Step 1.

Option 2: Examine a different piece of coin(s)/money from the same time, place, and culture that the original piece originated from, so that it is able to answer the same questions from Step 1.

Option 3: Create an original piece of coin(s)/money from a completely new and unique civilization that you have created. This piece of coin(s)/money must be able to fully answer the questions from Step 1.

Format(s)

When completing Step 2 of the analysis, you are only limited by your imagination in completing the piece. Some more popular formats include: drawings or models of coin(s), printed money, other traded goods, as well as others . . . **Go forth and create!**

Annotated Bibliography

Levenson, T. (2010). *Newton and the counterfeiter: The unknown detective career of the world's greatest scientist*. New York, NY: Mariner.

Abstract: This is a fantastic book weaving minted currency, history, and science. It is what a social studies book should be. Although it does not directly impact this instructional approach, it is a great book to have on hand. It describes how Newton assisted the Crown when counterfeiting was running rampant in England.

Mackay, J. (2010). *The world encyclopedia of coins and coin collecting*. London, England: Anness.

Abstract: This book is an essential reference for this instructional approach. It explains from the beginning how to collect coins and decipher currency. It is an invaluable resource for the social studies classroom.

Noles, J. (2009). *A pocketful of history: Four hundred years of America—one state quarter at a time*. New York, NY: De Capo.

Abstract: This book is a powerful resource for the introduction and whole-class activity portion of this instructional approach. It is also a substantial resource for students when they are tasked with designing their own coined currency.

General Rubric

	None (0%–29%)	Little (30%–59%)	Some (60%–89%)	Most (90%–100%)	Total Points
Structure/ Format	*No evidence of structure or format in product*	*Little evidence of structure or formatting*	*Evidence of some formatting*	*Most of the product is formatted*	
Research/ Analysis	*No evidence of student research or analysis*	*Little research or analysis present*	*Some evidence of research and analysis*	*Most of the product is researched and analyzed*	
Mechanics	*No proper use of mechanics present*	*Little use of proper mechanics*	*Some use of proper mechanics*	*Most of the product has proper mechanics*	
Ingenuity/ Creativity	*No evidence of ingenuity or creativity*	*Little use of ingenuity or creativity*	*Some evidence of ingenuity and creativity*	*Product filled with ingenuity and creativity*	
Presentation	*No presentation skills evident*	*Little presentation skills evident*	*Some presentation skills present*	*Presentation skills evident throughout*	
Final Score					
Comments/ Feedback					

Structure/Format

This portion of the rubric examines the physical structure of the students' product. Regardless of the media or the type of product, it must fit within the framework and guidelines established by the classroom teacher. The teacher should objectively address items such as the number of graphics, length of presentation, balance between verbal and visual content, and other features.

Research/Analysis

"Research" is the more objective of the two markers in this category of the rubric. The teacher can easily assess the students by looking at the number, quality, and frequency of citations in the students' products. This may seem at first somewhat rote in nature, but it helps to cultivate the students' knowledge and practice of research.

"Analysis" is more subjective. In order to effectively measure this particular marker, the classroom teacher must do a little. Examining the students' products closely, even reexamining them, the teacher should be able to find evidence of analysis in how cohesively the students connect their products to social studies, history, and the theme of each chapter.

Mechanics

In this portion of the rubric, the classroom teacher is assessing the students' command of the English language as evident in their products and presentation. The teacher will want to look at items such as spelling errors, grammar mistakes (e.g., fragments, run-ons, incomplete sentences, etc.), as well as other language mistakes. This is a good category to seek advice from an English/language arts colleague. Students who are not native English speakers should be assessed with this fact in mind.

Ingenuity/Creativity

This particular scoring category can do more to help the students' grades than harm. Although high scores in this category are not necessarily free, they can be somewhat more broad and generous. Just as "beauty is in the eye of the beholder," creativity and ingenuity are both understood differently by each individual. The classroom teacher who knows his or her students will be able to identify this category in the students' products.

Presentation

When assessing students' presentations, the teacher needs to look at the students' body language during the presentation, including eye contact, posture, and movement. Interaction with the audience is another factor to be considered. Most importantly, the students need to be able to coherently communicate the subject of their presentations in a manner that engages the audience and is easy for everyone to understand.

Scoring Categories

"None: 0%–29%"

If the students' product show little to nothing from the five grading categories listed vertically on the rubric, then it should be scored in this category. The "None" category is comprised of 0 to 29 percentage points. The classroom teacher will know best how to allocate points in regard to the students' products.

"Little: 30%–59%"

For the students to receive any points whatsoever in this particular scoring category, their products will have to show little evidence of any or all of the five grading categories.

"Some: 60%–89%"

Here, students display a solid working competency with a healthy measure of growth ahead of them in the grading categories. The teacher will more than likely find the majority of students settling comfortably in this scoring range.

"Most: 90%–100%"

This scoring range is for when the products hit most all of the requirements listed in the five grading categories. Again, the observant classroom teacher will be able to spot the products that hit this scoring category consistently. Rarely will all student products hit this scoring range throughout all five of the grading categories.

About the Author

R. Casey Davis, M. Ed., has been an educator since he was in high school. He has taught everything from elementary to college-level classes. When not preparing for the next lesson, he enjoys reading and writing, watching classic movies, and unconditionally cheering his favorite baseball teams. He currently resides in Chandler, AZ, with his wife and family. He graduated with his bachelor's degree from Texas Woman's University and his master's from the University of Houston-Victoria.

Common Core State Standards Alignment

Grade	Common Core State Standards
Grades 6–8	CCSS.ELA-Literacy.RH.6–8.1: Cite specific textual evidence to support analysis of primary and secondary sources.
	CCSS.ELA-Literacy.RH.6–8.2: Determine the central ideas or information of a primary or secondary source; provide an accurate summary of the source distinct from prior knowledge or opinions.
	CCSS.ELA-Literacy.RH.6–8.3: Identify key steps in a text's description of a process related to history/social studies (e.g., how a bill becomes law, how interest rates are raised or lowered).
	CCSS.ELA-Literacy.RH.6–8.4: Determine the meaning of words and phrases as they are used in a text, including vocabulary specific to domains related to history/social studies.
	CCSS.ELA-Literacy.RH.6–8.5: Describe how a text presents information (e.g., sequentially, comparatively, causally).
	CCSS.ELA-Literacy.RH.6–8.6: Identify aspects of a text that reveal an author's point of view or purpose (e.g., loaded language, inclusion or avoidance of particular facts).
	CCSS.ELA-Literacy.RH.6–8.7: Integrate visual information (e.g., in charts, graphs, photographs, videos, or maps) with other information in print and digital texts.

Grade	Common Core State Standards
Grades 6–8	CCSS.ELA-Literacy.RH.6–8.8: Distinguish among fact, opinion, and reasoned judgment in a text.
	CCSS.ELA-Literacy.RH.6–8.9: Analyze the relationship between a primary and secondary source on the same topic.
	CCSS.ELA-Literacy.RH.6–8.10: By the end of grade 8, read and comprehend history/social studies texts in the grades 6–8 text complexity band independently and proficiently.
Grades 9–10	CCSS.ELA-Literacy.RH.9–10.1: Cite specific textual evidence to support analysis of primary and secondary sources, attending to such features as the date and origin of the information.
	CCSS.ELA-Literacy.RH.9–10.2: Determine the central ideas or information of a primary or secondary source; provide an accurate summary of how key events or ideas develop over the course of the text.
	CCSS.ELA-Literacy.RH.9–10.3: Analyze in detail a series of events described in a text; determine whether earlier events caused later ones or simply preceded them.
	CCSS.ELA-Literacy.RH.9–10.4: Determine the meaning of words and phrases as they are used in a text, including vocabulary describing political, social, or economic aspects of history/social science.
	CCSS.ELA-Literacy.RH.9–10.5: Analyze how a text uses structure to emphasize key points or advance an explanation or analysis.
	CCSS.ELA-Literacy.RH.9–10.6: Compare the point of view of two or more authors for how they treat the same or similar topics, including which details they include and emphasize in their respective accounts.
	CCSS.ELA-Literacy.RH.9–10.7: Integrate quantitative or technical analysis (e.g., charts, research data) with qualitative analysis in print or digital text.
	CCSS.ELA-Literacy.RH.9–10.8: Assess the extent to which the reasoning and evidence in a text support the author's claims.
	CCSS.ELA-Literacy.RH.9–10.9: Compare and contrast treatments of the same topic in several primary and secondary sources.
	CCSS.ELA-Literacy.RH.9–10.10: By the end of grade 10, read and comprehend history/social studies texts in the grades 9–10 text complexity band independently and proficiently.